May
Everything
you wish be found
in your stocking
this Christmas

This book belongs to:

LEISURE ARTS, INC.
Little Rock, Arkansas

EDITORIAL STAFF

Vice President and Editor-in-Chief: Anne Van Wagner Childs. *Executive Director:* Sandra Graham Case. *Design Director:* Patricia Wallenfang Sowers. *Editorial Director:* Susan Frantz Wiles. *Publications Director:* Carla Bentley. *Creative Art Director:* Gloria Bearden. *Senior Graphics Art Director:* Melinda Stout. PRODUCTION — *Managing Editor:* Susan White Sullivan. *Senior Editor:* Andrea Ahlen. *Project Coordinators:* Carol Bowie Gifford, Joyce Scott Holland, and Jennifer S. Potts. EDITORIAL — *Managing Editor:* Linda L. Trimble. *Coordinating Editor:* Terri Leming Davidson. *Associate Editors:* Stacey Robertson Marshall and Janice Teipen Wojcik. ART — *Book/Magazine Graphics Art Director:* Diane M. Hugo. *Senior Graphics Illustrator:* Stephen L. Mooningham. *Graphics Illustrators:* Faith R. Lloyd, Fred Bassett, and Linda Culp Calhoun. *Photography Stylists:* Pam Choate, Sondra Daniel, Karen Hall, Aurora Huston, Courtney Frazier Jones, and Christina Myers. PROMOTIONS — *Managing Editors:* Alan Caudle and Marjorie Ann Lacy. *Associate Editors:* Steven M. Cooper, Dixie L. Morris, Ellen J. Clifton, and Debby Carr. *Designer:* Dale Rowett. *Art Director:* Linda Lovette Smart. *Publishing Systems Administrator:* Cindy Lumpkin. *Publishing Systems Assistants:* Susan M. Gray and Robert Walker.

BUSINESS STAFF

Publisher: Rick Barton. *Vice President and General Manager:* Thomas L. Carlisle. *Vice President, Finance:* Tom Siebenmorgen. *Vice President, Retail Marketing:* Bob Humphrey. *Vice President, National Accounts:* Pam Stebbins. *Retail Marketing Director:* Margaret Sweetin. *General Merchandise Manager:* Cathy Laird. *Vice President, Operations:* Brian U. Davis. *Distribution Director:* Rob Thieme. *Retail Customer Service Director:* Tonie B. Maulding. *Retail Customer Service Managers:* Carolyn Pruss and Wanda Price. *Print Production Manager:* Fred F. Pruss.

CREDITS

PHOTOGRAPHY: Ken West, Larry Pennington, Mark Mathews, Karen Shirey, and David Hale, Jr., of Peerless Photography, Little Rock, Arkansas; and Jerry R. Davis of Jerry Davis Photography, Little Rock, Arkansas. COLOR SEPARATIONS: Magna IV Color Imaging of Little Rock, Arkansas. CUSTOM FRAMING: Nelda and Carlton Newby of Creative Framers, North Little Rock, Arkansas. PHOTOGRAPHY LOCATIONS: The homes of Joan Adams, Dr. Dan and Sandra Cook, Barbara Denniston, and Dennis and Trisha Hendrix.

Library of Congress Catalog Number 98-65186
International Standard Book Number 1-57486-122-0

INTRODUCTION

Festive stockings hung on the mantel are as much a holiday tradition as the Christmas evergreen. The custom was founded with the famed generosity of St. Nicholas of Myra, a fourth-century bishop. According to legend, a poor Italian father was faced with selling one of his three daughters into slavery in order to afford the dowries needed for the others to marry. The good saint heard of the family's plight and, late one night, secretly tossed three bags of gold down the chimney. The bags miraculously fell into the sisters' stockings that were hanging by the fire to dry, thus saving the family from their fate. Today, children of all ages joyously hang their decorated stockings, anticipating the goodies that they'll discover on Christmas morn. Inside this complete volume of glorious stocking designs, you'll find styles befitting each member of the family. Select from vivid visions of St. Nick, jolly snowmen, and herald angels, or stitch a gentle Nativity or an old-time sampler. We've also included several coordinating projects for you to enjoy, such as cheerful ornaments, decorative pillows and afghans, and an elegant bellpull. So hang these enchanting stockings with care — and hope that St. Nicholas soon will be there!

3

TABLE OF CONTENTS

	PHOTO	CHART

THE HERALD ANGEL

In the midst of night so long ago, humble shepherds looked to the sky and beheld the splendor of God's celestial messenger. The angel blessed them with the jubilant news of the Savior's birth, echoed with a chorus of glad tidings. Evoking the joy of that first Noël, our heavenly host will bestow the glory of Christmas 'round about your home. The exquisite detail of her flowing cloak and feathery wings will beautifully enhance a wintry afghan, festive stocking, or special ornament. And through her beribboned elegance, she'll share wishes for peace, good will toward men.

CAROL

Chart on pages 40-43.

7

JOY TO THE WORLD

Accompanied by a joyful chorus, heaven and nature sang a welcoming herald on the Holy Night of Christ's birth. This stocking celebrates that joy in elegant Victorian style, with a cherub trumpeting the glory of His righteousness and fruited finery abounding in the wonder of His love. The splendid scene also offers fitting trims for an accent pillow or holiday sweater.

Chart on pages 44-47

A CHILD
IS BORN

Kneeling before the tiny King of Kings, the
Magi presented treasures of gold, frankincense
and myrrh — and founded the gift-giving celebration
of Christmas. Those riches not only lauded Christ's
birth, they also symbolized heaven's greatest gift to
mankind. Today we revere the glorious Nativity
with splendid creations hung by the fireside and
adornments tucked among evergreen branches.

Chart on pages 48-51

MERRY CHRISTMAS COUPLE

Our First Christmas

After weeks of hustle and bustle, the big moment has finally arrived! The sleigh is packed, the reindeer are harnessed, and Mrs. Claus is spending a rare and wondrous moment of calm with her jolly old gent before sending him off for an evening of chimney climbing. Portrayed on our merry door pillow and stocking, this jovial couple adds a tender touch to your first Christmas together — and many more to come.

Chart on pages 52-55

13

SANTA'S workshop

hidden away at the North Pole, Santa and his
troop of industrious elves keep his workshop abuzz
throughout the year. Happy hammers and busy brushes
add final touches to a wondrous world of playthings!
When the wish lists arrive at Christmastide, each
alphabet block, tiny train, and darling dolly is packed
into the sleigh, ready to tuck into a stocking or under
a tree. Then the load is whisked away into the arms
of delighted children around the world.

JESSIE

Chart on pages 56-59

15

Even little handmade touches make Yuletide
giving extra special! Brightly wrapped packages
feature a portrait of the jolly gent and unique
gift tags, while a whimsical stitched band
enhances a basket holding a diminutive tree.
With rows of merry peppermints, a clever
Advent calendar helps Santa count
off the days until the big night.

Chart on page 56

Chart on pages 56-57

Chart on pages 56-59

TO ALL A GOOD NIGHT

As good little children drift away to dreamland, St. Nick and his magical team soar above the housetops on their generous Yuletide journey. The nimble driver beckons each reindeer by name, urging them upward and onward to lightning speeds. Listen carefully on Christmas Eve, and you just might hear the patter of tiny hooves and the gentle thump of the sleigh on your roof. But the job will be done in barely a wink, and — as depicted on this cozy afghan and dreamy stocking — he'll dash away again, wishing "Happy Christmas to all, and to all a good night!"

BARBARA

Chart on pages 60-65

OPENING
his pack

In the final hours before his Christmas Eve trek,
old St. Nick opens his pack wide and fills it with every
imaginable toy. It's a magical bag, indeed, for it holds
treasures aplenty for children the world over! In goes
a cuddly teddy for Tim, a dainty doll for Donna, an
alphabet block for baby — and too many more to
count. Offering a glimpse of this bountiful scene,
our bright stocking will hold a generous share of
Santa's treats, and a matching card holder is a
clever keeper for the season's greetings.

Chart on pages 66-69

21

OLD-TIME SAMPLER

handmade samplers — cross stitched with love and care — are treasures that last a lifetime. A primer of heavenly stitches, a sampler stocking is highlighted with classic motifs and elegant trim. Portions of the sampler are repeated to create personalized cuffs for warm plaid stockings, along with an array of ornaments and accents. These homestyle touches will become beloved holiday heirlooms!

ELIZABETH

ABCDEFGHIJKLMN
abcdefghijklmnopqr

OPQRSTUVWXYZ
stuvwxyz 1234567890

Then the angel said, "Do not
be afraid, for behold, I bring
you good tidings of great joy which
will be to all people." Luke 2:10

Charts on pages 70-73

23

Chart on pages 70-71

24

*Joyful, all ye nations, rise,
Join the triumph of the skies;
With the angelic hosts proclaim,
"Christ is born in Bethlehem."*

Charts on pages 70-73

BENEVOLENT GENT

With kind eyes and a gentle gesture to hush anyone who spies his arrival, Santa Claus comes soundlessly to deliver tokens to wishful boys and girls. Only in dreams should the benevolent gent be seen, but on this magical eve, the anticipation of his visit will keep even the sleepiest eyes open. There is time to catch but a glimpse of him at his elusive work, though, for he vanishes just as quickly as he appears.

Chart on pages 74-75

FATHER CHRISTMAS

Red-breasted birds on berried evergreens
mark the path as Father Christmas presses
onward through his busiest night. Bearing a
pack overflowing with treasures, the kindly
hooded patriarch also totes a sparkling tree to
its destination. This holiday traveler, bundled
in fur-trimmed cape and sporting a flowing
white beard, reflects early European
images of our beloved gift-giver.

Chart on pages 76-77

29

SANTAS AROUND THE WORLD

his scarlet suit and rosy cheeks may be a familiar
sight to us, but Santa often appears quite differently
to children in other lands. He may don a long,
crimson coat or rustic robe, and his festive cap might
be replaced with a hood and sprigs of holly. Instead
of toys for good girls and boys, his bag may be full of
twigs for naughty tykes. Our assortment of diminutive
stockings celebrates the many faces of this benevolent
soul. For whether he's St. Nick or Père Noël, he
is still the beloved gentleman who embodies
the generosity of the season.

Charts on pages 78-81

BOTANICAL
BEAUTIES

$\mathcal{D}$ressed in crimson, the florals of Christmas
bring joy to the heart of winter in a vibrant
splash of color. The evergreen holly symbolizes
Christ's gift of eternal life, and the handsome
poinsettia is said to have bloomed on the night
of His birth. These woodsy emblems of the
season add a festive touch to elegant
stockings and a handsome container.

Charts on page 88

33

childhood pleasures

Christmas is a time of joyous pleasures for little ones, when bright eyes and genuine smiles await the arrival of a jolly old elf bringing delightful gifts for one and all. With restless anticipation, children hang their special stockings in hopes that the roomy gift-holders will be brimming with glorious goodies by morning's light.

Charts on pages 82-83 and 86

For little children everywhere;
A joyous season still we make;
We bring our precious gifts to them,
Even for the dear child Jesus' sake.

— PHOEBE CARY

Chart on pages 82-83.

36

Chart on pages 84-85

MR. SNOWMAN
AND FRIENDS

Ah — that first snowfall of the Christmas season! With a thick blanket of downy white flakes covering the ground, mitten-clad children burst outside, full of smiles and laughter. A gentle flurry floats from the sky as they work with great care to sculpt the perfect snowman — complete with a hat and pipe borrowed from Dad's closet! This tender scene is captured in a pair of stockings that will surely bring back fond memories of snow-filled childhood days.

Chart on pages 90-91

the herald angel

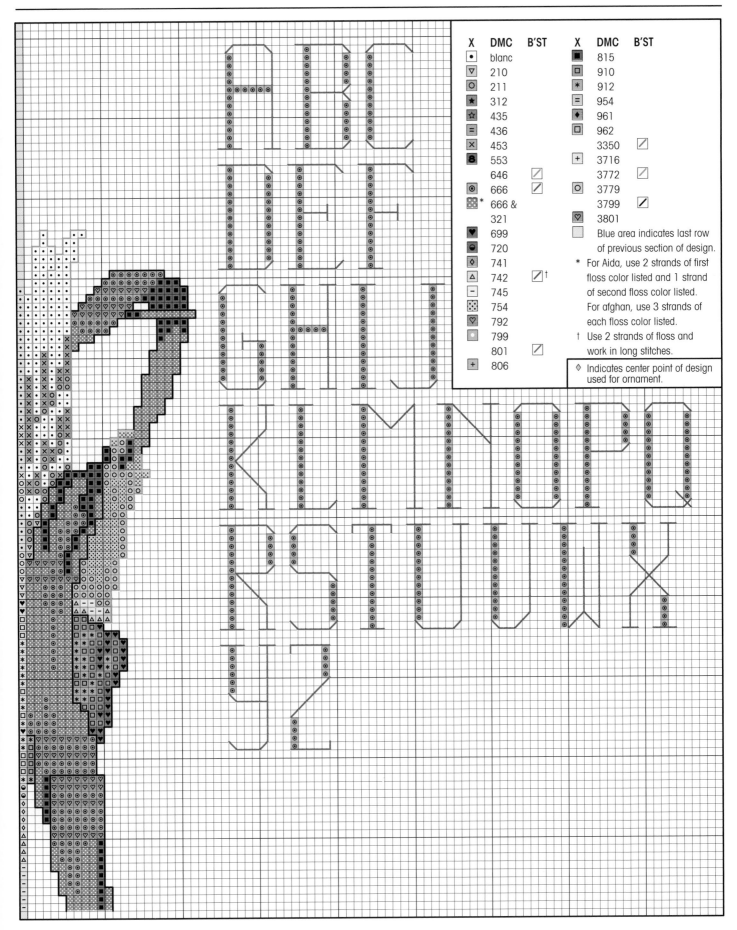

X	DMC	B'ST		X	DMC	B'ST
•	blanc			■	815	
▽	210			▣	910	
○	211			✳	912	
★	312			=	954	
☆	435			◆	961	
⊟	436			▢	962	
✕	453				3350	╱
❽	553			+	3716	
	646	╱			3772	╱
⊙	666	╱		○	3779	
▨*	666 &				3799	╱
	321			♡	3801	
❤	699				Blue area indicates last row	
◖	720				of previous section of design.	
◇	741			*	For Aida, use 2 strands of first	
△	742	╱†			floss color listed and 1 strand	
–	745				of second floss color listed.	
▨	754				For afghan, use 3 strands of	
▽	792				each floss color listed.	
▢	799			†	Use 2 strands of floss and	
	801	╱			work in long stitches.	
+	806					

◇ Indicates center point of design
used for ornament.

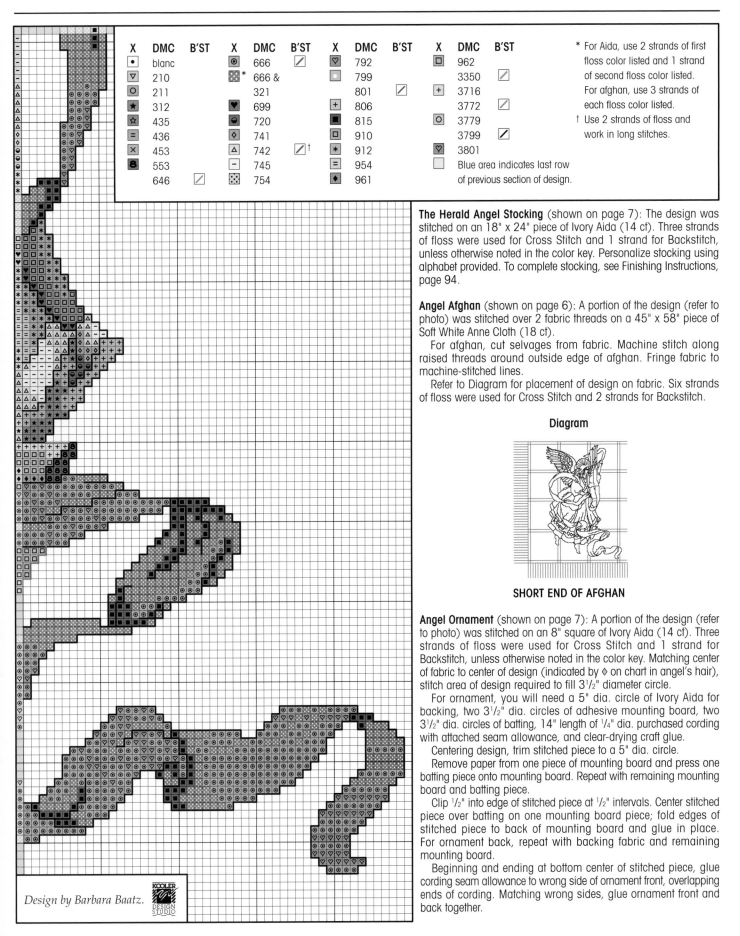

X	DMC	B'ST	X	DMC	B'ST	X	DMC	B'ST	X	DMC	B'ST
•	blanc		◉	666	◥	▽	792		◻	962	
▽	210		▨*	666 &		◻	799			3350	◥
◯	211			321			801	◥	+	3716	
★	312		♥	699		+	806			3772	◥
☆	435		◐	720		■	815		◯	3779	
=	436		◇	741		◻	910			3799	◥
✕	453		△	742	◥†	*	912		▽	3801	
❽	553		–	745		=	954				
	646	◥	▨	754		◆	961		◻	Blue area indicates last row of previous section of design.	

* For Aida, use 2 strands of first floss color listed and 1 strand of second floss color listed. For afghan, use 3 strands of each floss color listed.

† Use 2 strands of floss and work in long stitches.

The Herald Angel Stocking (shown on page 7): The design was stitched on an 18" x 24" piece of Ivory Aida (14 ct). Three strands of floss were used for Cross Stitch and 1 strand for Backstitch, unless otherwise noted in the color key. Personalize stocking using alphabet provided. To complete stocking, see Finishing Instructions, page 94.

Angel Afghan (shown on page 6): A portion of the design (refer to photo) was stitched over 2 fabric threads on a 45" x 58" piece of Soft White Anne Cloth (18 ct).

For afghan, cut selvages from fabric. Machine stitch along raised threads around outside edge of afghan. Fringe fabric to machine-stitched lines.

Refer to Diagram for placement of design on fabric. Six strands of floss were used for Cross Stitch and 2 strands for Backstitch.

Diagram

SHORT END OF AFGHAN

Angel Ornament (shown on page 7): A portion of the design (refer to photo) was stitched on an 8" square of Ivory Aida (14 ct). Three strands of floss were used for Cross Stitch and 1 strand for Backstitch, unless otherwise noted in the color key. Matching center of fabric to center of design (indicated by ◇ on chart in angel's hair), stitch area of design required to fill 3½" diameter circle.

For ornament, you will need a 5" dia. circle of Ivory Aida for backing, two 3½" dia. circles of adhesive mounting board, two 3½" dia. circles of batting, 14" length of ¼" dia. purchased cording with attached seam allowance, and clear-drying craft glue.

Centering design, trim stitched piece to a 5" dia. circle.

Remove paper from one piece of mounting board and press one batting piece onto mounting board. Repeat with remaining mounting board and batting piece.

Clip ½" into edge of stitched piece at ½" intervals. Center stitched piece over batting on one mounting board piece; fold edges of stitched piece to back of mounting board and glue in place. For ornament back, repeat with backing fabric and remaining mounting board.

Beginning and ending at bottom center of stitched piece, glue cording seam allowance to wrong side of ornament front, overlapping ends of cording. Matching wrong sides, glue ornament front and back together.

Design by Barbara Baatz.

KOOLER DESIGN STUDIO

43

center name

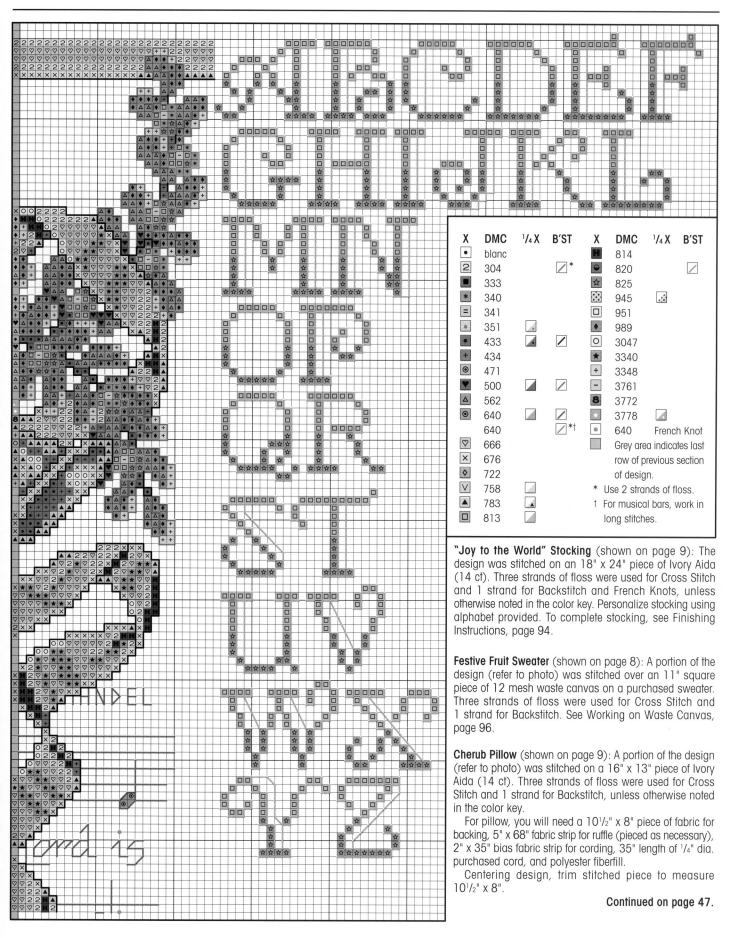

X	DMC	¼ X	B'ST		X	DMC	¼ X	B'ST
•	blanc				H	814		
2	304	◨	◹*		◓	820		◹
■	333				☆	825		
✳	340				⊞	945		⊡
=	341				◻	951		
⦁	351	◸			◆	989		
◉	433	◸	◹		O	3047		
+	434				★	3340		
◉	471				+	3348		
♥	500	◸	◹		-	3761		
△	562				8	3772		
◉	640	◸	◹		◉	3778		◸
	640		◹*†		•	640		French Knot
♡	666				▨	Grey area indicates last		
✕	676					row of previous section		
◇	722					of design.		
V	758	◸			*	Use 2 strands of floss.		
▲	783	◸			†	For musical bars, work in		
◻	813	◸				long stitches.		

"Joy to the World" Stocking (shown on page 9): The design was stitched on an 18" x 24" piece of Ivory Aida (14 ct). Three strands of floss were used for Cross Stitch and 1 strand for Backstitch and French Knots, unless otherwise noted in the color key. Personalize stocking using alphabet provided. To complete stocking, see Finishing Instructions, page 94.

Festive Fruit Sweater (shown on page 8): A portion of the design (refer to photo) was stitched over an 11" square piece of 12 mesh waste canvas on a purchased sweater. Three strands of floss were used for Cross Stitch and 1 strand for Backstitch. See Working on Waste Canvas, page 96.

Cherub Pillow (shown on page 9): A portion of the design (refer to photo) was stitched on a 16" x 13" piece of Ivory Aida (14 ct). Three strands of floss were used for Cross Stitch and 1 strand for Backstitch, unless otherwise noted in the color key.

For pillow, you will need a 10½" x 8" piece of fabric for backing, 5" x 68" fabric strip for ruffle (pieced as necessary), 2" x 35" bias fabric strip for cording, 35" length of ¼" dia. purchased cord, and polyester fiberfill.

Centering design, trim stitched piece to measure 10½" x 8".

Continued on page 47.

JOY TO THE WORLD

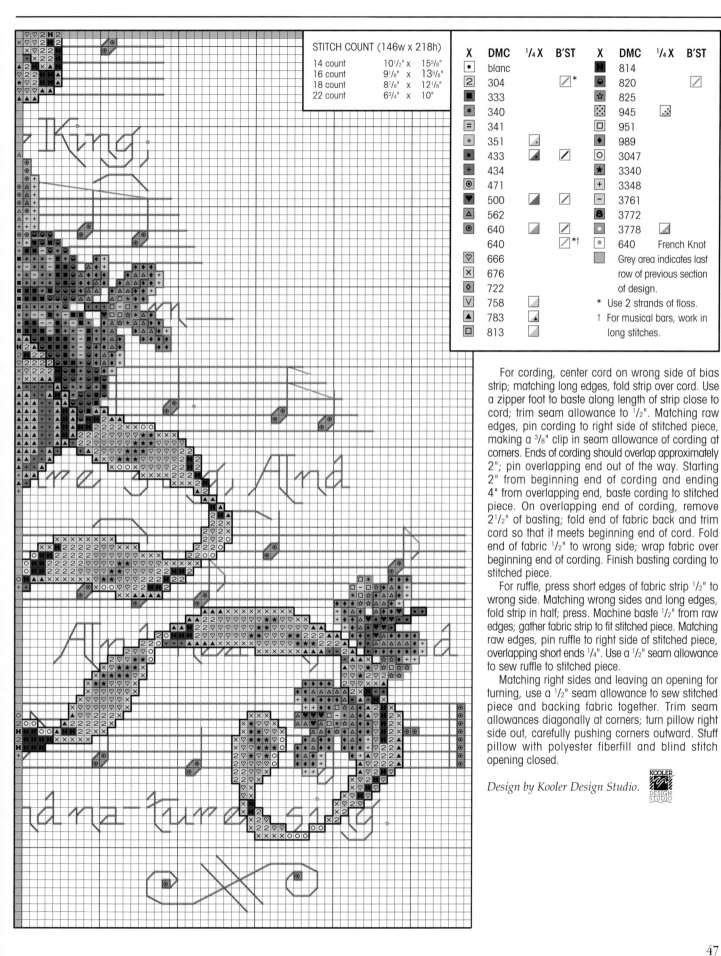

STITCH COUNT (146w x 218h)

14 count	10½"	x	15⅝"
16 count	9⅛"	x	13⅝"
18 count	8⅛"	x	12⅛"
22 count	6¾"	x	10"

X	DMC	¼ X	B'ST	X	DMC	¼ X	B'ST
•	blanc			H	814		
2	304		╱ *	◓	820		╱
■	333			☆	825		
*	340			⊞	945	⬚	
=	341			□	951		
⊙	351	◸		◆	989		
◕	433	◸	╱	○	3047		
+	434			★	3340		
⊚	471			+	3348		
♥	500	◺	╱	−	3761		
▲	562			8	3772		
⊙	640	◺	╱	◦	3778	◺	
	640		╱ *†	◦	640	French Knot	
♡	666				Grey area indicates last		
✕	676				row of previous section		
◈	722				of design.		
V	758	◺			* Use 2 strands of floss.		
▲	783	◣			† For musical bars, work in		
□	813	◺			long stitches.		

For cording, center cord on wrong side of bias strip; matching long edges, fold strip over cord. Use a zipper foot to baste along length of strip close to cord; trim seam allowance to ½". Matching raw edges, pin cording to right side of stitched piece, making a ⅜" clip in seam allowance of cording at corners. Ends of cording should overlap approximately 2"; pin overlapping end out of the way. Starting 2" from beginning end of cording and ending 4" from overlapping end, baste cording to stitched piece. On overlapping end of cording, remove 2½" of basting; fold end of fabric back and trim cord so that it meets beginning end of cord. Fold end of fabric ½" to wrong side; wrap fabric over beginning end of cording. Finish basting cording to stitched piece.

For ruffle, press short edges of fabric strip ½" to wrong side. Matching wrong sides and long edges, fold strip in half; press. Machine baste ½" from raw edges; gather fabric strip to fit stitched piece. Matching raw edges, pin ruffle to right side of stitched piece, overlapping short ends ¼". Use a ½" seam allowance to sew ruffle to stitched piece.

Matching right sides and leaving an opening for turning, use a ½" seam allowance to sew stitched piece and backing fabric together. Trim seam allowances diagonally at corners; turn pillow right side out, carefully pushing corners outward. Stuff pillow with polyester fiberfill and blind stitch opening closed.

Design by Kooler Design Studio.

KOOLER DESIGN STUDIO

a child is born

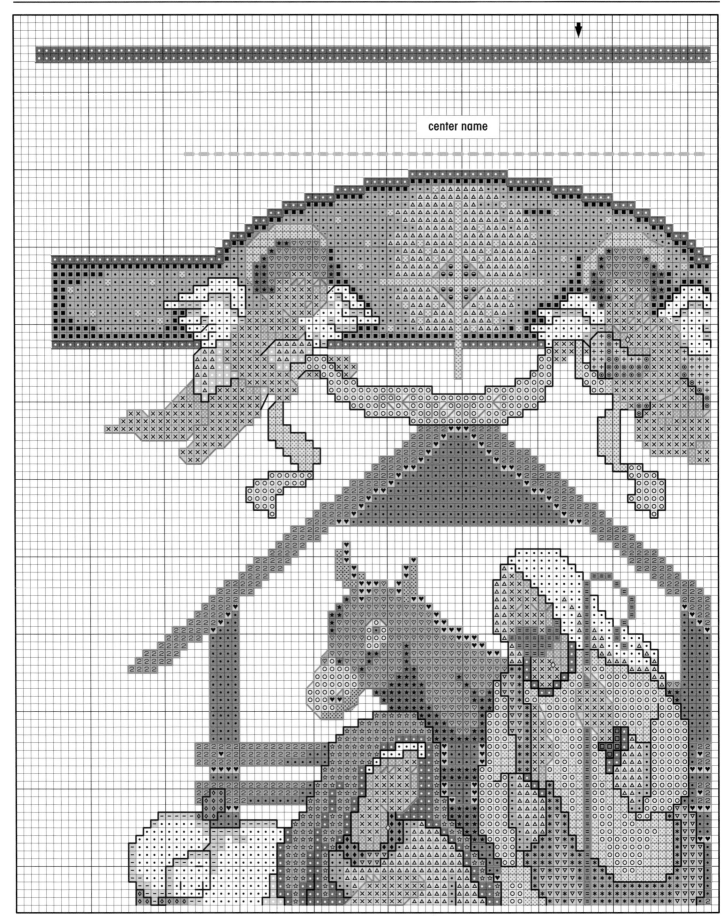

center name

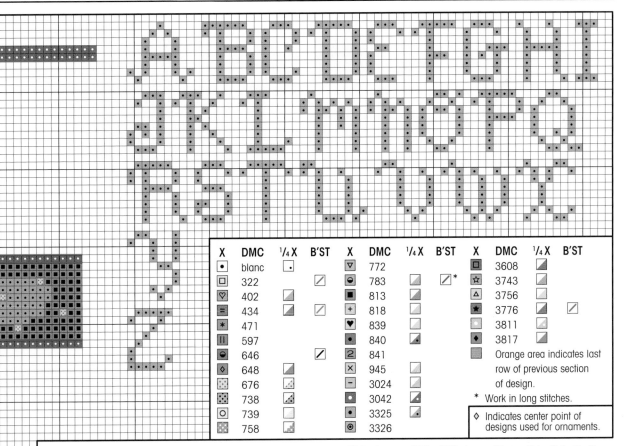

X	DMC	¼ X	B'ST	X	DMC	¼ X	B'ST	X	DMC	¼ X	B'ST
•	blanc			▽	772			▣	3608		
□	322	◢		◓	783	◢	◢*	☆	3743	◢	
♥	402	◢		■	813	◢		△	3756	◢	
▤	434	◢	◢	+	818	◢		★	3776	◢	◢
✳	471			♥	839	◢		○	3811		
‖	597			●	840	◢		◆	3817	◢	
◐	646	◢		2	841						
◇	648	◢		✕	945	◢					
∷	676	◢		−	3024	◢					
▦	738	◢		○	3042	◢					
○	739			•	3325	◢					
▦	758	◢		◉	3326						

Orange area indicates last row of previous section of design.

* Work in long stitches.

◇ Indicates center point of designs used for ornaments.

A Child Is Born Stocking (shown on page 11): The design was stitched on an 18" x 24" piece of Ivory Aida (14 ct). Three strands of floss were used for Cross Stitch and 1 strand for Backstitch. Personalize stocking using alphabet provided. To complete stocking, see Finishing Instructions, page 94.

"Rejoice" Stocking (shown on page 11): A portion of the design (refer to photo) was stitched on a 20" x 13" piece of Ivory Aida (14 ct). Three strands of floss were used for Cross Stitch and 1 strand for Backstitch. Personalize stocking using alphabet provided.

For stocking, you will need a 17½" x 7" piece of fabric for cuff backing, two 14" x 20" pieces of fabric for stocking, two 14" x 20" pieces of fabric for lining, 2" x 5" piece of fabric for hanger, tracing paper, and fabric marking pencil.

For stocking cuff, center design horizontally and allow a 2" margin at top of design; trim stitched piece to measure 17½" x 7". Matching right sides and short edges, fold stitched piece in half. Using a ½" seam allowance, sew short edges together. Repeat for cuff backing. Matching right sides, raw edges, and seams, use a ½" seam allowance to sew cuff and cuff backing together along lower edge of cuff; turn right side out and press. Baste cuff and cuff backing together close to raw edges.

For stocking pattern, match arrows of Stocking Pattern, page 94, to form one pattern and trace pattern onto tracing paper; add a ½" seam allowance on all sides and cut out pattern. Matching right sides and raw edges, place stocking fabric pieces together; place pattern on fabric pieces and pin pattern in place. Use fabric marking pencil to draw around pattern; remove pattern and cut out on drawn line. Repeat with lining fabric pieces.

Matching right sides and leaving top edge open, use a ½" seam allowance to sew stocking pieces together. Clip seam allowance at curves and turn stocking right side out.

Matching right sides and leaving top edge open, use a ⅝" seam allowance to sew lining pieces together; trim seam allowance close to stitching. **Do not turn lining right side out.** With wrong sides facing, place lining inside stocking. Baste stocking and lining together close to raw edges.

Referring to photo and matching raw edges, place right side of cuff to inside of stocking with cuff back seam at center back of stocking. Use a ½" seam allowance to sew cuff and stocking together. Fold cuff 5" to outside of stocking and press.

For hanger, press each long edge of fabric strip ½" to center. Matching long edges, fold strip in half and sew close to folded edges. Fold hanger in half, matching short edges; refer to photo and blind stitch to inside of stocking.

Nativity Ornaments (shown on page 10): Portions of the design (refer to photo) were each stitched on a 6" square of Ivory Aida (14 ct). Three strands of floss were used for Cross Stitch and 1 strand for Backstitch. They were inserted in purchased gold oval frames (2¼" x 2½" opening). Matching center of frame opening to center of design (indicated by ◇ on chart), stitch area of design required to fill frame opening.

Design by Kooler Design Studio.

a child is born

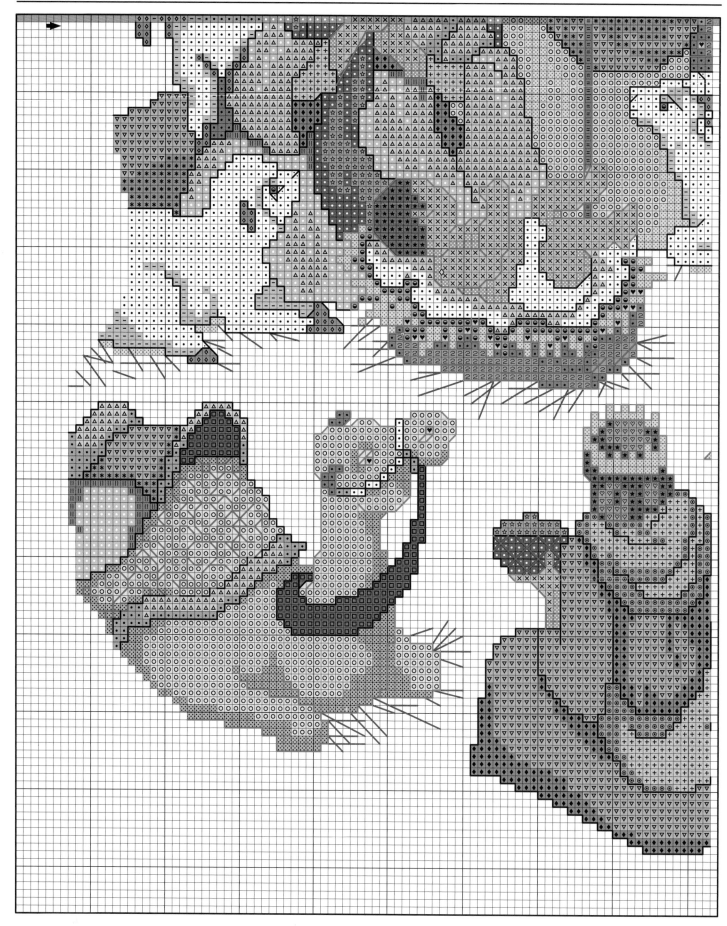

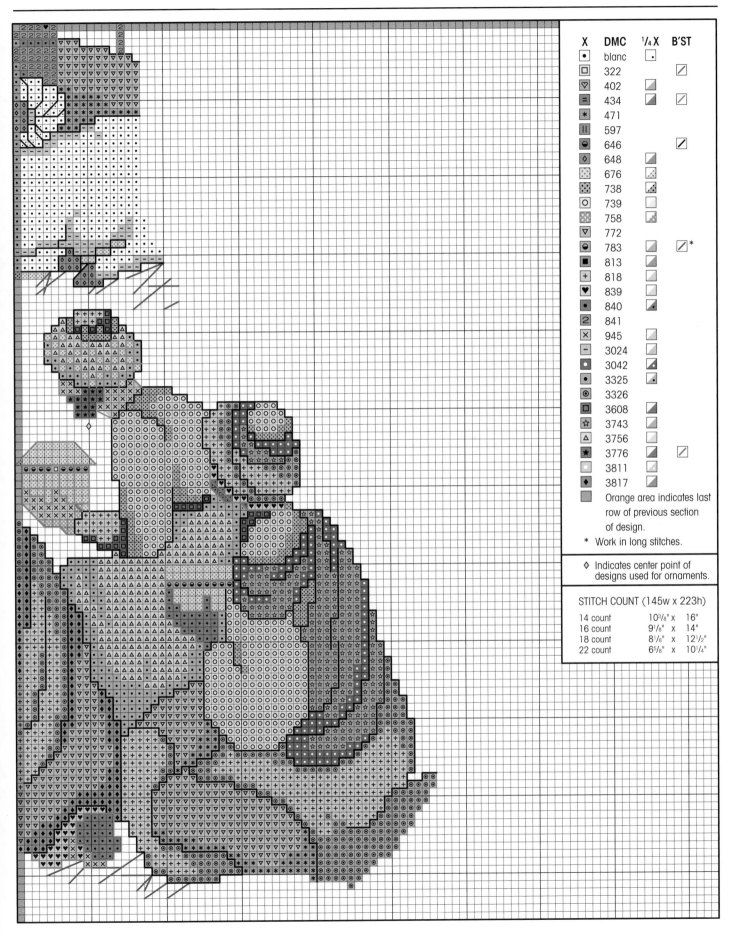

X	DMC	¼X	B'ST
•	blanc	•	
▢	322		◿
♡	402	◢	
=	434	◢	◿
✳	471		
‖	597		
◓	646		◿
◇	648	◢	
▨	676	◢	
▨	738	◢	
○	739	◢	
▨	758	◢	
▽	772		
◓	783	◢	◿*
■	813	◢	
+	818	◢	
♥	839	◢	
●	840	◢	
2	841		
✕	945	◢	
−	3024	◢	
▣	3042	◢	
•	3325	◢	
◉	3326		
▢	3608	◢	
☆	3743	◢	
△	3756	◢	
★	3776	◢	◿
○	3811	◢	
◆	3817	◢	
▨	Orange area indicates last row of previous section of design.		

* Work in long stitches.

◊ Indicates center point of designs used for ornaments.

STITCH COUNT (145w x 223h)

14 count	10⅜"	x	16"
16 count	9⅛"	x	14"
18 count	8⅛"	x	12½"
22 count	6⅝"	x	10¼"

MERRY CHRISTMAS COUPLE

STITCH COUNT (115w x 194h)

count			
14 count	8¼"	x	13⅞"
16 count	7¼"	x	12⅛"
18 count	6½"	x	10⅞"
22 count	5¼"	x	8⅞"

center name

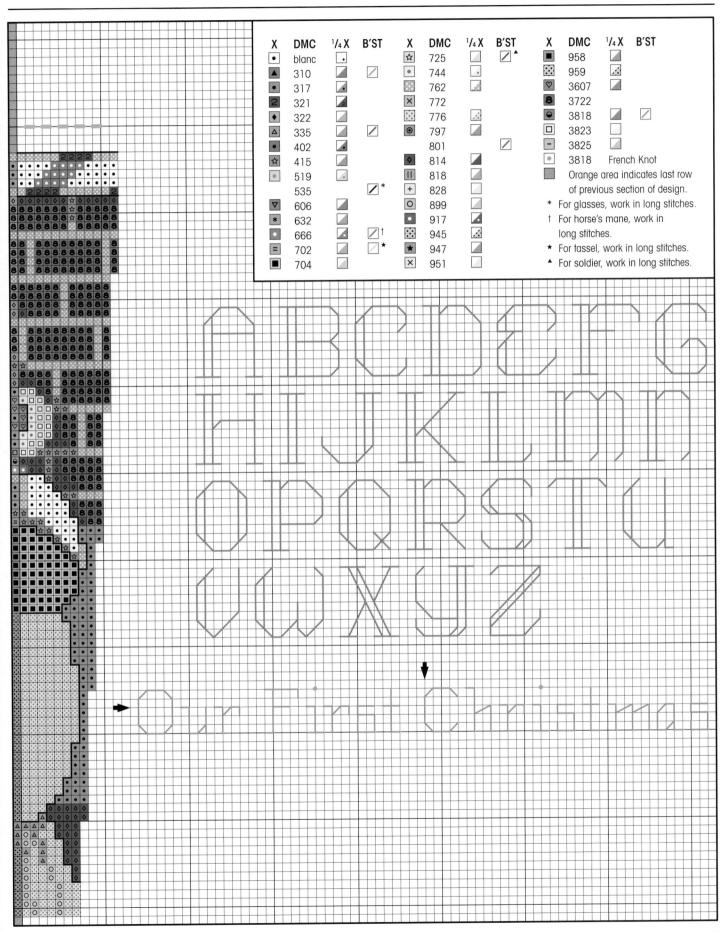

X	DMC	1/4 X	B'ST		X	DMC	1/4 X	B'ST		X	DMC	1/4 X	B'ST
•	blanc				☆	725				■	958		
▲	310				•	744				▨	959		
•	317				▨	762				♡	3607		
2	321				×	772				8	3722		
♦	322				▨	776				⊖	3818		
△	335				⊙	797				☐	3823		
●	402					801				-	3825		
☆	415				◆	814				●	3818	French Knot
●	519				‖	818					Orange area indicates last row
	535		*		+	828					of previous section of design.
▽	606				○	899				*	For glasses, work in long stitches.
✳	632				●	917				†	For horse's mane, work in
●	666		†		▨	945					long stitches.
=	702		*		★	947				★	For tassel, work in long stitches.
■	704				×	951				▲	For soldier, work in long stitches.

ABCDEFG
HIJKLMN
OPQRSTU
VWXYZ

Our First Christmas

53

MERRY CHRISTMAS COUPLE

Merry Christmas Couple Stocking (shown on page 13): The design was stitched over 2 fabric threads on an 18" x 24" piece of Antique White Lugana (25 ct). Three strands of floss were used for Cross Stitch and 1 strand for Backstitch. Personalize stocking using alphabet provided, page 53. To complete stocking, see Finishing Instructions, page 94.

"Our First Christmas" Pillow (shown on page 12): A portion of the design (refer to photo) was stitched on a 12" square of Antique White Aida (14 ct). Three strands of floss were used for Cross Stitch, 1 strand for Backstitch, and 2 strands for Backstitch lettering and French Knots. Center lettering (page 53) horizontally with top of letters 4 squares below bottom of design.

For pillow, you will need an 8½" square piece of fabric for pillow backing, 34" length of ¼" dia. purchased cording with attached seam allowance, two 18" lengths of ⅜"w ribbon for hanger, and polyester fiberfill.

Centering design, trim stitched piece to measure 8½" square.

If needed, trim seam allowance of cording to ½"; pin cording to right side of stitched piece, making a ⅜" clip in seam allowance of cording at corners. Ends of cording should overlap approximately 4". Turn overlapped ends of cording toward outside edge of stitched piece; baste cording to stitched piece.

Matching right sides and raw edges, pin stitched piece and backing fabric together. Leaving an opening for turning, use a ½" seam allowance to sew pillow front and backing fabric together. Trim seam allowances diagonally at corners; turn pillow right side out, carefully pushing corners outward. Stuff pillow with polyester fiberfill and blind stitch opening closed.

For hanger, refer to photo and tack one length of ribbon to each upper corner of pillow back; tie hanger in a bow.

Design by Linda Gillum.

center name

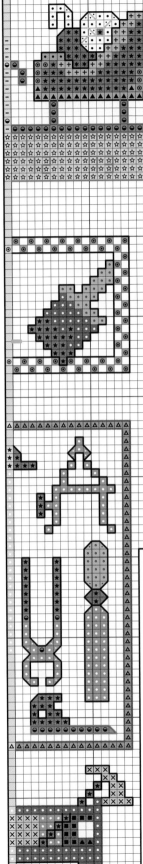

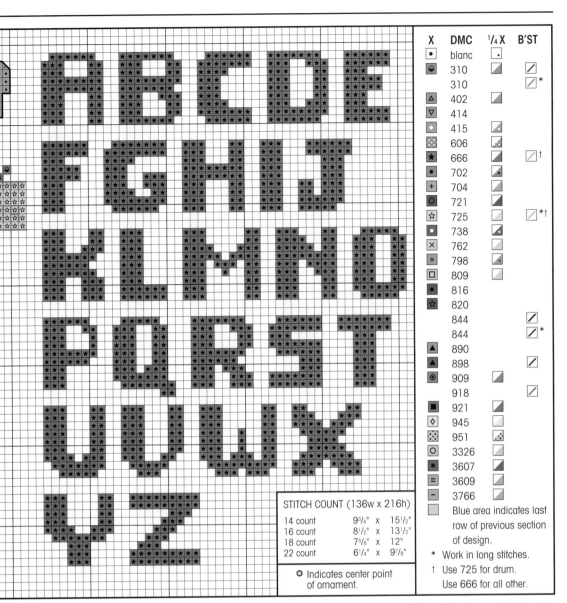

X	DMC	¼ X	B'ST
•	blanc	•	
◉	310	◢	◢
	310		◢*
▲	402	◢	
▽	414		
◙	415	◢	
▦	606	◢	
★	666	◢	◢†
•	702	◢	
◙	721	◢	
☆	725	◢	◢*†
◙	738	◢	
×	762	◢	
◉	798	◢	
□	809	◢	
●	816		
☆	820		
	844		◢
	844		◢*
▲	890		
▲	898		◢
◉	909	◢	
	918		◢
■	921	◢	
◇	945	◢	
▦	951	◢	
◙	3326	◢	
✳	3607	◢	
≡	3609	◢	
–	3766	◢	
▨			Blue area indicates last row of previous section of design.

* Work in long stitches.
† Use 725 for drum.
  Use 666 for all other.

STITCH COUNT (136w x 216h)

14 count	9¾"	x	15½"
16 count	8½"	x	13½"
18 count	7⅝"	x	12"
22 count	6¼"	x	9⅞"

◎ Indicates center point of ornament.

Santa's Workshop Stocking (shown on page 15): The design was stitched on an 18" x 24" piece of White Aida (14 ct). Three strands of floss were used for Cross Stitch and 1 strand for Backstitch. Personalize stocking using alphabet provided. To complete stocking, see Finishing Instructions, page 94.

Santa's Workshop Advent Calendar (shown on page 17): A portion of the design (refer to photo) was stitched on a 15" x 23" piece of White Aida (14 ct). Three strands of floss were used for Cross Stitch and 1 strand for Backstitch. Center design horizontally and stitch with top of design 4½" from one short edge of fabric.

For calendar, you will need 24 cellophane-wrapped candies, fabric glue, ½ yard of low-loft batting, ¾ yard of 44/45"w fabric, thread to match fabric, 2 yards of ⅝"w grosgrain ribbon, 7⅜ yards of 1/16"w satin ribbon, and a chenille needle.

Note: Use a ½" seam allowance for all seams.

For calendar front, trim stitched piece to measure 11" x 19" with top of design 2½" from top edge. For fabric borders, cut two 3¼" x 11" strips of fabric. Matching right sides and raw edges, sew one strip to each short edge of stitched piece. Press seam allowances toward strips. Cut two 3¼" x 23½" strips of fabric. Matching right sides and raw edges, sew one strip to each long edge of stitched piece and attached strips. Press seam allowances toward strips.

For inside ribbon border, cut three 10" lengths of grosgrain ribbon. Glue one length each at top and bottom of stitched piece directly along inside of fabric border. For center ribbon border, glue ribbon 1¾" below bottom of design. Cut two 18" lengths of grosgrain ribbon. Glue one length to each long side of stitched piece directly along inside of fabric border.

For candy ties, cut twenty-four 11" lengths of satin ribbon. Referring to photo, lay candies on calendar to determine ribbon placement. For each candy tie, thread needle with one satin ribbon length and thread through Aida at determined point. Repeat for remaining candy ties.

For backing, cut a piece of fabric same size as calendar front. Cut a piece of batting same size as backing fabric. Matching right sides and raw edges, place backing fabric on calendar front; place batting on backing fabric. Beginning at bottom edge and leaving an opening for turning, sew all three layers together. Trim batting seam allowance close to stitching; trim corners diagonally. Turn right side out, carefully pushing corners outward. Blind stitch opening closed.

For hanging sleeve, cut a 3½" x 13½" piece of fabric. Press all edges ¼" to wrong side; machine stitch pressed edges

Continued on page 59.

santa's workshop

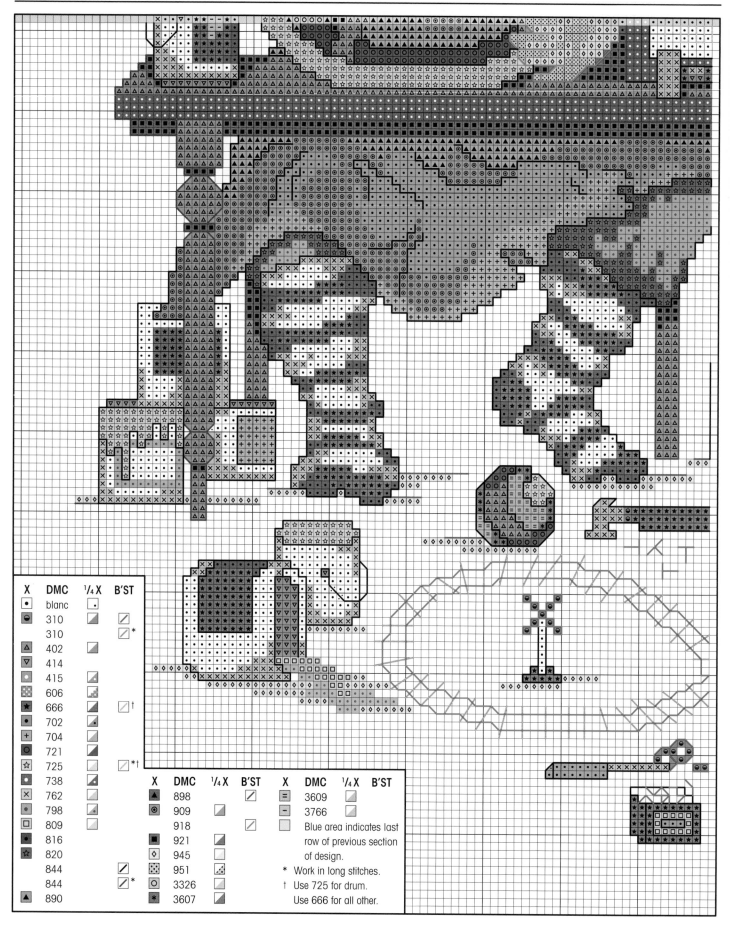

X	DMC	¼ X	B'ST
•	blanc	•	
◒	310	◢	◩
	310		◩*
▲	402	◢	
▽	414		
◉	415	◢	
▦	606	◢	
★	666	◢	◩†
●	702	◢	
+	704	◢	
◎	721	◢	
☆	725	◢	◩*†
◨	738	◢	
✕	762	◢	
◦	798	◢	
▢	809	◢	
◼	816	◢	
✩	820	◢	
	844	◩	
	844	◩*	
▲	890		

X	DMC	¼ X	B'ST	X	DMC	¼ X	B'ST
▲	898		◩	=	3609	◢	
◉	909	◢		–	3766	◢	
	918		◩	▢	Blue area indicates last		
◼	921	◢			row of previous section		
◇	945	◢			of design.		
	951	⬚		*	Work in long stitches.		
◯	3326	◢		†	Use 725 for drum.		
✹	3607	◢			Use 666 for all other.		

58

in place. With one long edge of hanging sleeve ¼" below top of calendar; pin hanging sleeve to backing. Whipstitch long edges of hanging sleeve to backing.

Tie each candy in place; trim ribbon ends as desired.

Santa Face Gift Bag (shown on page 16): A portion of the design (refer to photo) was stitched on a 5" x 6" piece of White Aida (14 ct). Three strands of floss were used for Cross Stitch and 1 strand for Backstitch. Matching center of pattern to center of design (indicated by ○ on chart), stitch area of design required to fill pattern.

For gift bag, you will need a 3" x 4" piece of adhesive mounting board, tracing paper, pencil, 3" x 4" piece of batting, 13" length of ¼" dia. purchased cording with attached seam allowance, 20" length of ¼"w ribbon for bow, 20mm jingle bell, clear-drying craft glue, 7" x 9" gift bag, 6" x 8" piece of fabric, and fusible web.

For ornament, trace pattern onto tracing paper; cut out pattern. Draw around pattern once on mounting board and once on batting; cut out. Remove paper from mounting board and press batting piece onto mounting board.

Referring to photo, position pattern on wrong side of stitched piece; pin pattern in place. Cut stitched piece **1" larger** than pattern on all sides. Clip ½" into edge of stitched piece at ½" intervals. Center wrong side of stitched piece over batting on mounting board piece; fold edges of stitched piece to back of mounting board and glue in place.

Beginning and ending at top center of stitched piece, glue cording seam allowance to wrong side of ornament front, overlapping ends of cording. Tie ribbon in a bow and glue to top of ornament. Glue bell to bottom of ornament.

For gift bag, follow manufacturer's instructions to fuse web to wrong side of fabric piece. Cut fabric piece into an oval shape approximately 1" larger than ornament; fuse to center front of bag. Centering ornament over fabric piece, glue ornament in place.

Santa Face Ornament (shown on page 14): Refer to Santa Face Gift Bag instructions above to make ornament front. (You will not need gift bag, fabric, or fusible web.)

You will also need a 5" x 6" piece of White Aida for backing, 3" x 4" piece of adhesive mounting board, and 3" x 4" piece of batting.

For ornament back, use pattern and cut one each from mounting board and batting. Remove paper from mounting board and press batting piece onto mounting board. Cut backing fabric **1" larger** than pattern on all sides. Clip ½" into edge of backing fabric at ½" intervals. Center backing fabric over batting on mounting board piece; fold edges of backing fabric to back of mounting board and glue in place. Match wrong sides and glue ornament front and back together.

Santa's Workshop Gift Tags (shown on page 16): A portion of the design (refer to photo) was stitched on an 8" x 4" piece of White Aida (16 ct). Two strands of floss were used for Cross Stitch and 1 strand for Backstitch. Personalize gift tag using alphabet provided, page 57.

For each gift tag, you will need an 8" x 4" piece of lightweight white fabric for backing, fabric stiffener, small foam brush, hole punch, and a 4" length of ⅛"w ribbon.

Apply a heavy coat of fabric stiffener to wrong side of stitched piece using small foam brush. Matching wrong sides, place stitched piece on backing fabric, smoothing stitched piece while pressing fabric pieces together; allow to dry. Apply fabric stiffener to backing fabric; allow to dry. Cut out close to edges of stitched design. Referring to photo, use hole punch to cut hole in left side of gift tag. Thread ribbon through hole.

Toy Basket Band (shown on page 16): A portion of the design (refer to photo) was stitched on a 30" x 6" piece of White Aida (16 ct). Two strands of floss were used for Cross Stitch and 1 strand for Backstitch.

For basket, you will need an 8" dia. terra-cotta flowerpot, 1 yard of 44/45"w fabric, sewing thread, polyester fiberfill, and craft glue.

Measure flowerpot from rim to rim, taking tape measure underneath flowerpot; add 12". Cut a circle determined diameter from fabric.

Using a double thickness of sewing thread, baste around fabric circle 6" from edge. Place an even thickness of polyester fiberfill inside basting line. Center flowerpot on fiberfill. Gently pull basting threads until fabric is gathered snugly around rim of flowerpot; knot ends to secure. Turn edge of fabric to wrong side, tucking edge inside basting thread. Glue to rim of flowerpot at basting line.

Centering design, trim stitched piece to measure 29" x 5".

Matching right sides and long edges, fold stitched piece in half. Use a ½" seam allowance to sew long edges together; turn stitched piece right side out. With seam centered in back, press stitched piece flat. Press short edges ½" to wrong side.

Referring to photo, glue stitched piece around flowerpot, covering basting line.

Design by Kooler Design Studio.

TO ALL A GOOD NIGHT

STITCH COUNT (173w x 276h)

14 count	12³/₈" x	19³/₄"
16 count	10⁷/₈" x	17¹/₄"
18 count	9⁵/₈" x	15³/₈"
22 count	7⁷/₈" x	12⁵/₈"

center name

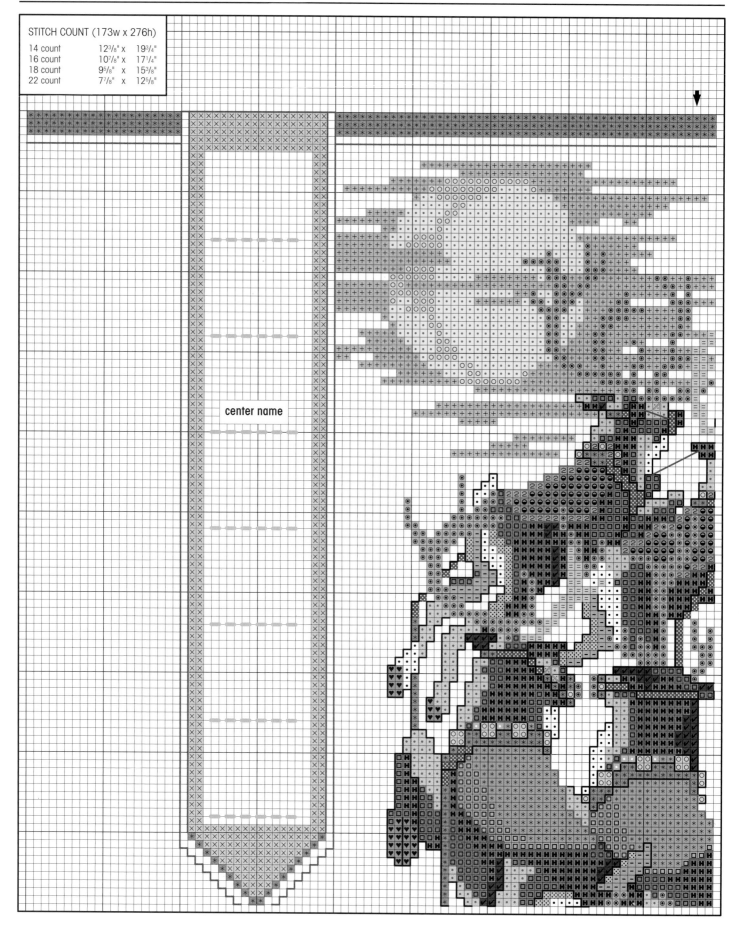

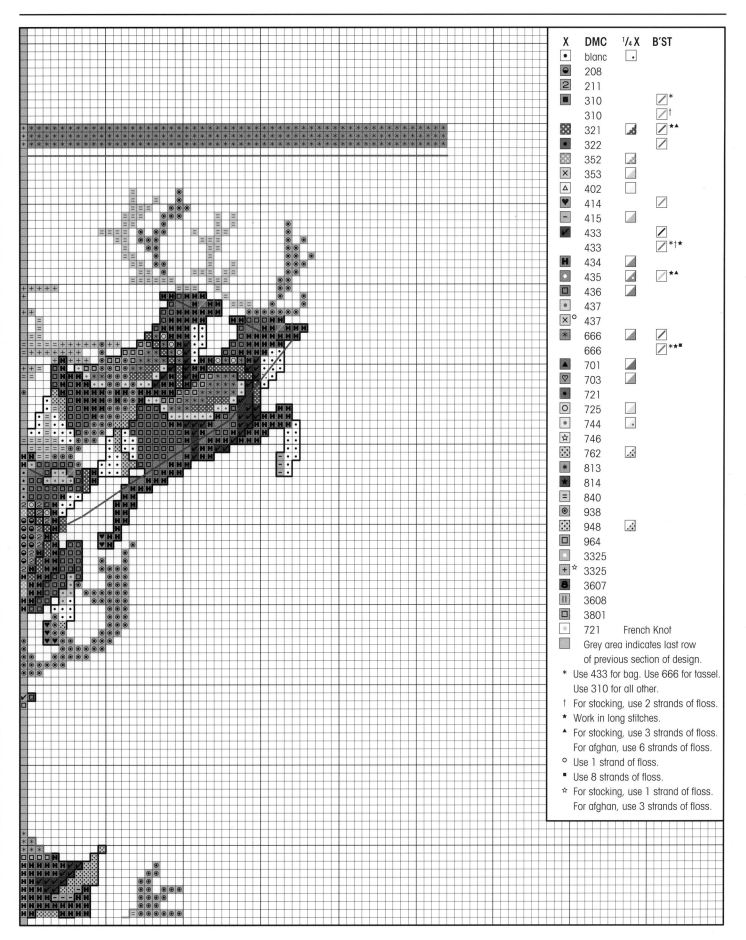

X	DMC	¼ X	B'ST
•	blanc	·	
◕	208		
2	211		
■	310	◢	⟋*
	310		⟋†
▨	321	◢	⟋★▲
◉	322		⟋
▨	352	◢	
✕	353	◢	
△	402	□	
♥	414		⟋
-	415	◢	
◪	433		⟋
	433		⟋*†★
H	434	◢	
◉	435	◢	⟋★▲
▢	436	◢	
◦	437		
✕°	437		
✳	666	◢	⟋
	666		⟋*★■
▲	701	◢	
♡	703	◢	
●	721		
○	725	□	
◦	744		·
☆	746		
▨	762	◢	
✳	813		
★	814		
=	840		
◉	938		
▨	948	◢	
▢	964		
◦	3325		
+☆	3325		
8	3607		
II	3608		
▢	3801		
◦	721	French Knot	

Grey area indicates last row of previous section of design.

* Use 433 for bag. Use 666 for tassel. Use 310 for all other.
† For stocking, use 2 strands of floss.
★ Work in long stitches.
▲ For stocking, use 3 strands of floss. For afghan, use 6 strands of floss.
° Use 1 strand of floss.
■ Use 8 strands of floss.
☆ For stocking, use 1 strand of floss. For afghan, use 3 strands of floss.

TO ALL A GOOD NIGHT

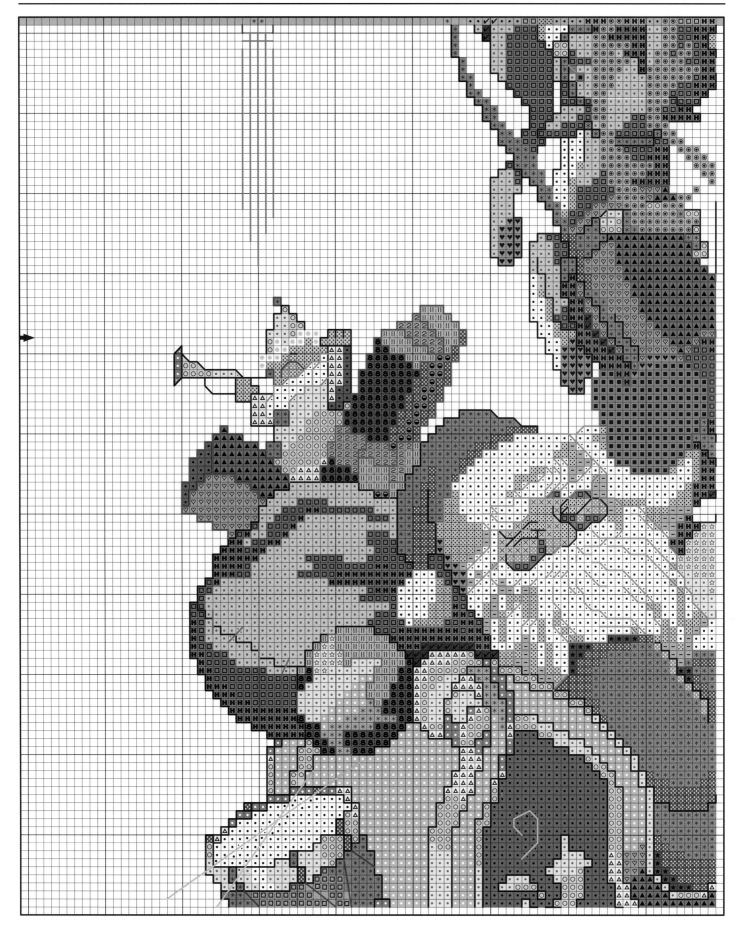

X	DMC	1/4 X	B'ST	X	DMC	1/4 X	B'ST
•	blanc	•		☆	746		
◖	208			▨	762	▨	
2	211			*	813		
■	310		╱ *	★	814		
	310		╱ †	=	840		
▨	321	▨	╱ ★▲	⊙	938		
●	322		╱	▨	948	▨	
▨	352	▨		▢	964		
×	353	◺		○	3325		
△	402	▢		+ ☆	3325		
♥	414		╱	8	3607		
-	415	◺		II	3608		
▨	433		╱	▢	3801		
	433		╱ *†★	○	721	French Knot	
H	434	◺					
○	435	◺	╱ ★▲				
▢	436	◺					
•	437						
×°	437						
▨	666	◺	╱				
	666		╱ **■				
▲	701	◺					
▽	703	◺					
●	721						
○	725	◺					
•	744	•					

Grey area indicates last row of previous section of design.

* Use 433 for bag. Use 666 for tassel. Use 310 for all other.

† For stocking, use 2 strands of floss.

★ Work in long stitches.

▲ For stocking, use 3 strands of floss. For afghan, use 6 strands of floss.

° Use 1 strand of floss.

■ Use 8 strands of floss.

☆ For stocking, use 1 strand of floss. For afghan, use 3 strands of floss.

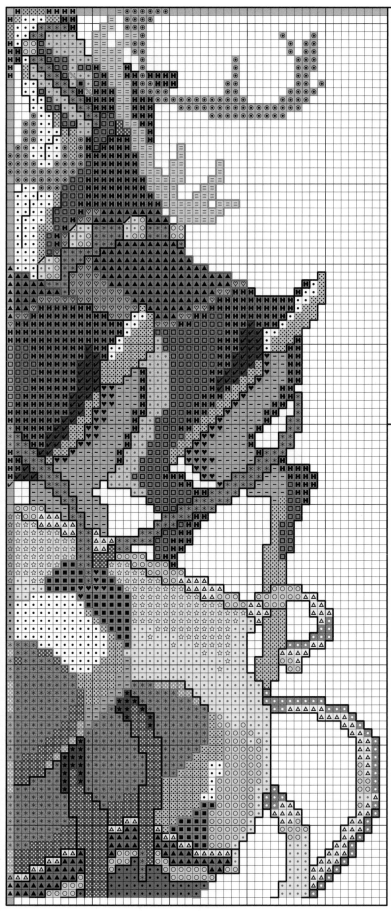

To All a Good Night Stocking (shown on page 19): The design was stitched on an 18" x 24" piece of Ivory Aida (18 ct). Two strands of floss were used for Cross Stitch and 1 strand for Backstitch and French Knots, unless otherwise noted in the color key. Personalize stocking using alphabet provided. Lengthen or shorten banner as needed. Fill in remaining background of banner using 1 strand of DMC 437 floss. To complete stocking, see Finishing Instructions, page 94.

Santa and Sleigh Afghan (shown on page 18): A portion of the design (refer to photo) was stitched over 2 fabric threads on a 45" x 58" piece of Royal Blue Anne Cloth (18 ct). Six strands of floss were used for Cross Stitch and French Knots and 2 strands for Backstitch, unless otherwise noted in the color key. Refer to Diagram (page 65) for placement of design on afghan.

For afghan binding, you will need approximately 6 yards of 2½"w bias fabric strips (pieced as necessary) and a fabric marking pencil.

Cut selvages from fabric. For rounded corners, use a circular shape for a pattern and mark corners of fabric with fabric marking pencil; cut fabric along drawn lines.

For binding, fold fabric strip in half lengthwise with wrong sides together; press. Fold one long edge of fabric strip ½" to wrong side; press. Matching raw edges, pin binding to right side of afghan. Ends of binding should overlap approximately 1". On overlapping end of binding, fold fabric ½" to wrong side; wrap fabric over beginning end of binding. Using a ½" seam allowance, sew binding to afghan. Fold binding to wrong side of afghan; pin pressed edge in place, covering stitching line. Blind stitch binding to afghan; press.

Design by Kooler Design Studio.

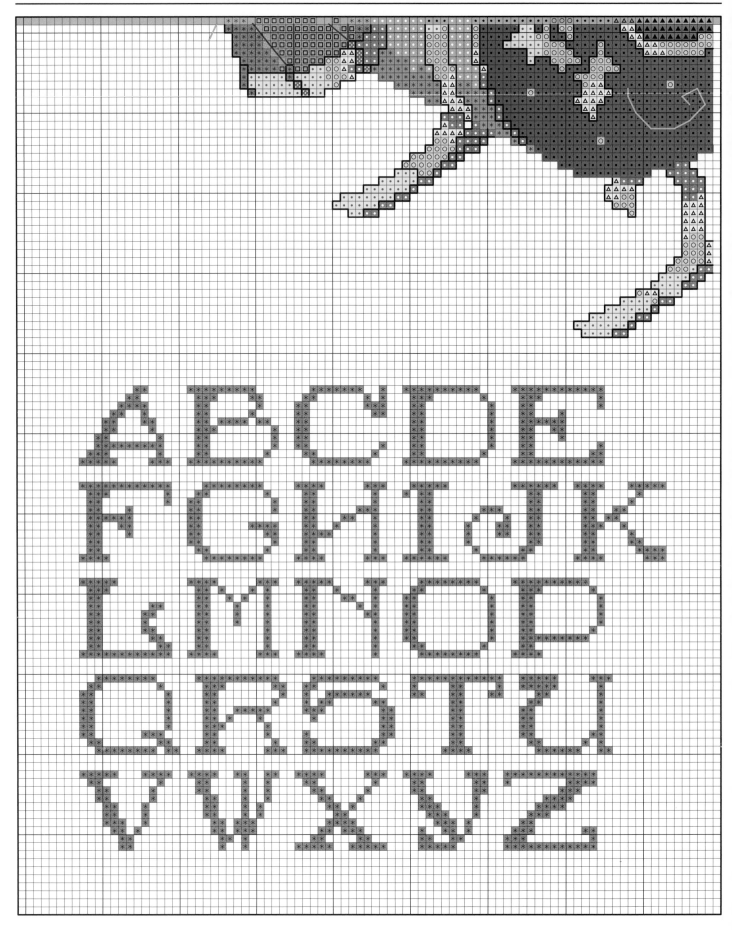

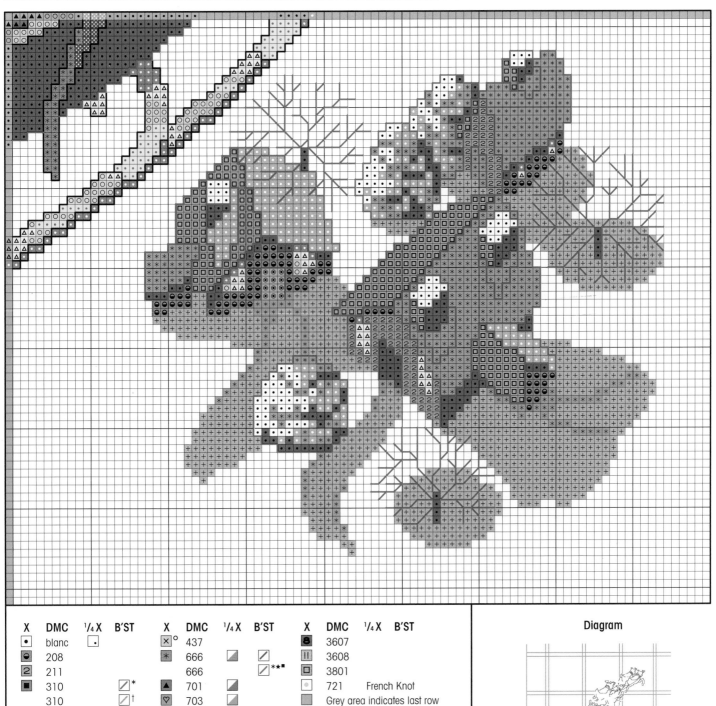

X	DMC	¼X	B'ST	X	DMC	¼X	B'ST	X	DMC	¼X	B'ST
•	blanc	•		×°	437			❽	3607		
◐	208			✳	666	◣	◹	‖	3608		
2	211				666		◹ ★★■	▢	3801		
■	310		◹ *	▲	701	◹		○	721		French Knot
	310		◹ †	♡	703	◹		▨	Grey area indicates last row		
▨	321	◪	◹ ★▲	●	721	◹			of previous section of design.		
●	322		◹	○	725	◸		*	Use 433 for bag. Use 666 for tassel.		
▨	352	◪		•	744		•		Use 310 for all other.		
×	353	◢		☆	746			†	For stocking, use 2 strands of floss.		
△	402	◻		▦	762	◳		★	Work in long stitches.		
♥	414		◹	✳	813			▲	For stocking, use 3 strands of floss.		
–	415	◢		★	814				For afghan, use 6 strands of floss.		
✔	433		◹	=	840			°	Use 1 strand of floss.		
	433		◹ *†★	◉	938			■	Use 8 strands of floss.		
H	434	◢		▦	948	◳		☆	For stocking, use 1 strand of floss.		
●	435	◢	◹ ★▲	▢	964				For afghan, use 3 strands of floss.		
▢	436	◢		●	3325						
•	437			+	3325 ☆						

Diagram

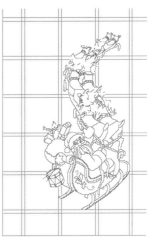

SHORT END OF AFGHAN

OPENING his pack

STITCH COUNT (116w x 195h)

14 count	8³/₈"	x	14"
16 count	7¹/₄"	x	12¹/₄"
18 count	6¹/₂"	x	10⁷/₈"
22 count	5³/₈"	x	8⁷/₈"

66

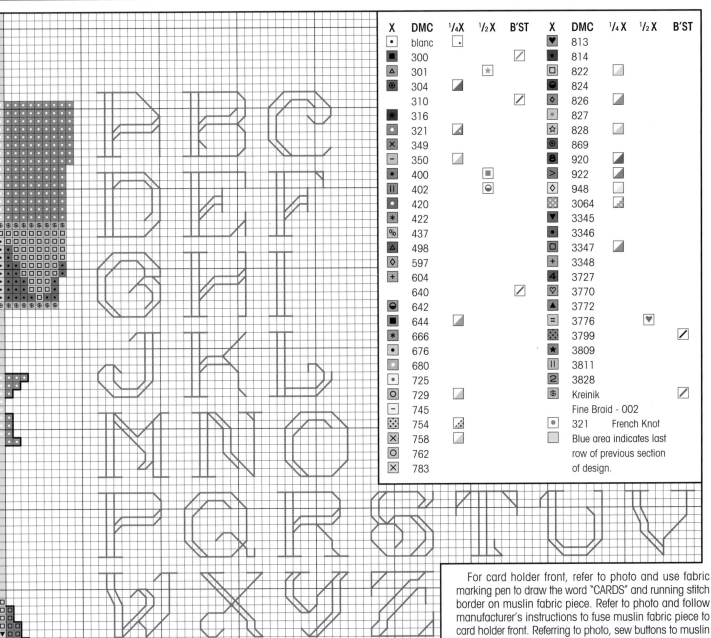

X	DMC	1/4X	1/2X	B'ST	X	DMC	1/4X	1/2X	B'ST
•	blanc	•			♥	813			
■	300		/		•	814			
△	301		★		□	822		/	
⊙	304	/			●	824			
	310		/		◇	826	/		
★	316				•	827			
◘	321	/			☆	828		/	
✕	349				◉	869			
-	350	/			8	920	/		
•	400		■		➤	922	/		
‖	402		⊖		◇	948	/		
●	420				▦	3064	/		
*	422				▼	3345			
△	437				•	3346			
%	498				□	3347		/	
◇	597				+	3348			
+	604				4	3727			
	640		/		♡	3770			
●	642				▲	3772			
■	644	/			=	3776		♥	
*	666				▦	3799			/
•	676				★	3809			
•	680				‖	3811			
•	725				2	3828			
○	729	/			$	Kreinik			/
-	745					Fine Braid - 002			
▦	754	▦			⊙	321 French Knot			
✕	758	/			▢	Blue area indicates last			
○	762					row of previous section			
✕	783					of design.			

For card holder front, refer to photo and use fabric marking pen to draw the word "CARDS" and running stitch border on muslin fabric piece. Refer to photo and follow manufacturer's instructions to fuse muslin fabric piece to card holder front. Referring to photo, sew buttons to muslin fabric piece at corners.

Matching right sides and leaving top edge open, use a 1/2" seam allowance to sew card holder front and back together. Trim seam allowances diagonally at corners; turn card holder right side out. Press top edge of card holder 1 1/2" to wrong side.

Matching right sides and leaving top edge open, use a 5/8" seam allowance to sew lining pieces together; trim seam allowance close to stitching. **Do not turn lining right side out.** Press top edge of lining 1 1/2" to wrong side.

For hangers, fold each ribbon in half; referring to photo and aligning hangers with pegs on frame, pin hangers to inside of card holder back. Whipstitch hangers in place. With wrong sides facing, place lining inside card holder; blind stitch lining to card holder.

Design by Nancy Rossi.

Opening His Pack Stocking (shown on page 21): The design was stitched on a 16" x 22" piece of Ivory Aida (14 ct). Three strands of floss were used for Cross Stitch and 1 strand for Half Cross Stitch, Backstitch, and French Knots. After completing DMC 321 border at top of design, use alphabet provided to personalize stocking, positioning letters on dashed line.

For stocking, you will need a 16" x 22" piece of fabric for backing, two 16" x 22" pieces of fabric for lining, 38" length of 1/4" dia. purchased cording with attached seam allowance, 2" x 6" piece of fabric for hanger, tracing paper, and fabric marking pencil. To complete stocking, see Finishing Instructions, page 95.

St. Nick Card Holder (shown on page 20): A portion of the design (refer to photo) was stitched on a 15" x 13" piece of Ivory Aida (14 ct). Three strands of floss were used for Cross Stitch and 1 strand for Half Cross Stitch, Backstitch, and French Knots. It was inserted in a 10 3/4" x 8" purchased peg frame (8 3/4" x 5" opening).

For card holder, you will need two 11 1/2" x 13" pieces of fabric for front and back, two 11 1/2" x 13" pieces of fabric for lining, an 8 1/4" x 3 3/4" piece of muslin, fabric marking pen, paper-backed fusible web, 4 buttons, and four 8" lengths of 1/4"w ribbon for hangers.

OPENING HIS PACK

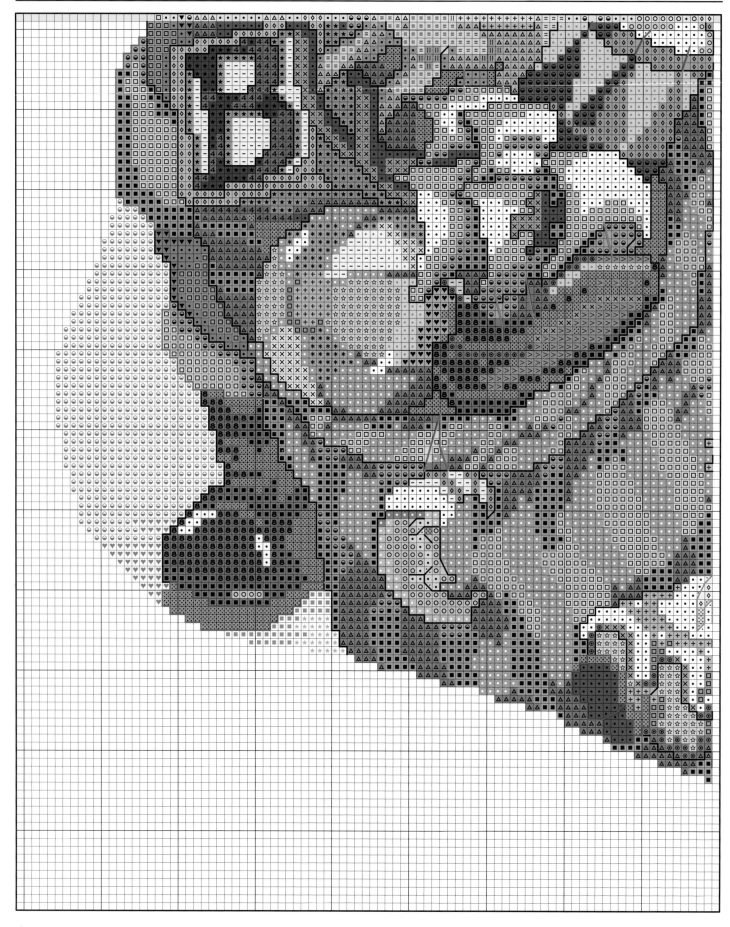

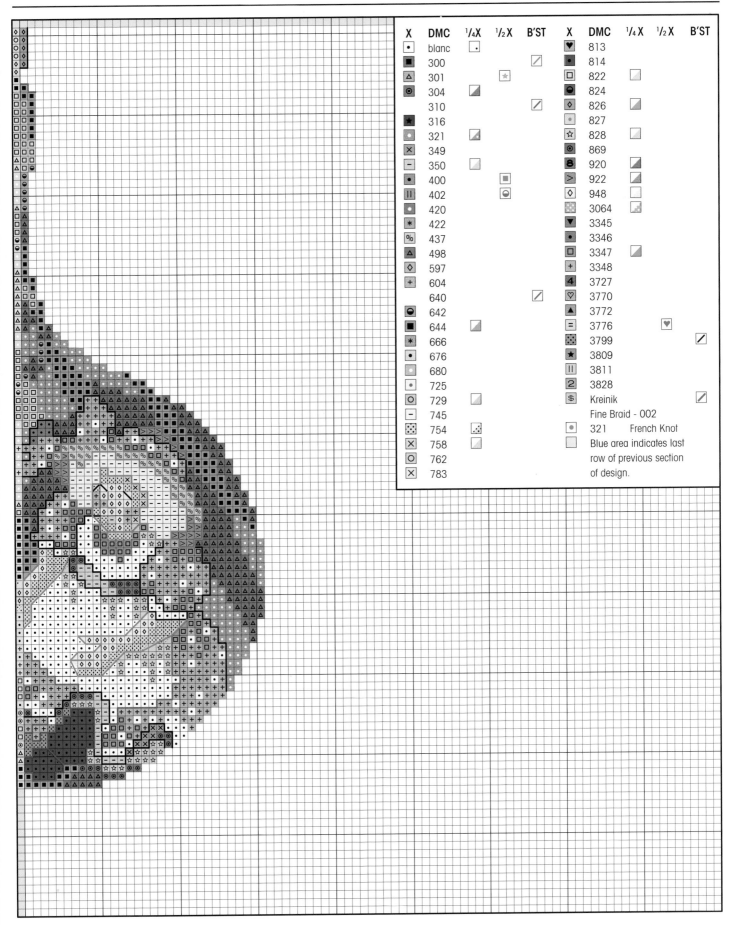

X	DMC	¼X	½X	B'ST	X	DMC	¼X	½X	B'ST
•	blanc	·			♥	813			
■	300			/	•	814			
△	301		★		□	822			
⊙	304	◢			◒	824			
	310			/	◇	826	◢		
★	316				•	827			
◉	321	◢			☆	828			
×	349				◉	869			
–	350	◢			8	920		◢	
•	400		■		>	922		◢	
‖	402		◒		◇	948			
•	420				▦	3064		◪	
∗	422				▼	3345			
%	437				•	3346			
△	498				□	3347	◢		
◇	597				+	3348			
+	604				4	3727			
	640			/	♡	3770			
◒	642				▲	3772			
■	644	◢			=	3776		♥	
∗	666				⋰	3799			/
•	676				★	3809			
•	680				‖	3811			
•	725				②	3828			
○	729	◢			$	Kreinik			/
–	745					Fine Braid - 002			
⋰	754	⋰			•	321	French Knot		
×	758	◢			▢	Blue area indicates last			
○	762					row of previous section			
×	783					of design.			

OLD-TIME SAMPLER

center name

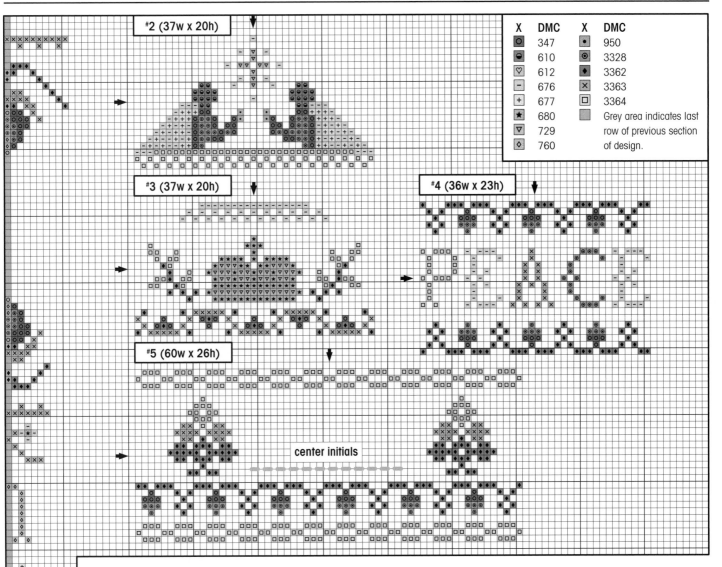

#2 (37w x 20h)

#3 (37w x 20h)

#4 (36w x 23h)

#5 (60w x 26h)

center initials

X	DMC	X	DMC
◉	347	•	950
◓	610	◎	3328
▽	612	◆	3362
−	676	✕	3363
+	677	▢	3364
★	680	▨	Grey area indicates last
▽	729		row of previous section
◇	760		of design.

Old-time Sampler Stocking (shown on page 23): Design #1 was stitched over 2 fabric threads on an 18" x 24" piece of Cream Cashel Linen® (28 ct). Three strands of floss were used for Cross Stitch. Personalize stocking using DMC 680 floss and upper case alphabet from chart. To complete stocking, see Finishing Instructions, page 94.

Sampler Border Stocking (shown on page 24): A portion of Design #1 (refer to photo) was stitched over 2 fabric threads on an 8" x 22" piece of Cream Cashel Linen® (28 ct). Three strands of floss were used for Cross Stitch. Personalize cuff using DMC 680 floss and upper case alphabet from chart. To complete stocking, see Finishing Instructions, page 94.

Floral Border Shaker Boxes (shown on page 25): Portions of Design #1 (refer to photo) were each stitched over 2 fabric threads on a 4" high piece of Cream Belfast Linen (32 ct). To determine length of fabric piece, measure around outside of lid and add 4". Two strands of floss were used for Cross Stitch.

For each box, you will need a Shaker box in desired shape and size, tracing paper, pencil, fabric to cover top of lid, fabric marking pencil, and clear-drying craft glue.

For pattern, trace around box lid onto tracing paper; add ³/₄" on all sides and cut out. Position pattern on fabric and cut out. Clip

¹/₄" into edge of fabric at 1" intervals. Center fabric on lid; fold edge of fabric down and glue to side of lid.

Centering design, trim stitched piece to measure 2" longer and 1" wider than lid measurements.

On one long edge, turn stitched piece ¹/₂" to wrong side and press. Repeat with remaining raw edges. Referring to photo, glue stitched piece to side of lid.

Sampler Border Basket Band (shown on page 25): A portion of Design #1 (refer to photo) was stitched over 2 fabric threads on a 34" x 6" piece of Cream Cashel Linen® (28 ct). Repeat design until stitched piece measures approximately 30" in length. Three strands of floss were used for Cross Stitch.

For basket, you will need a 10" dia. basket with handle, 1¹/₈ yards of fabric, sewing thread, polyester fiberfill, and craft glue.

Measure basket from rim to rim, taking tape measure underneath basket; add 16". Cut a circle determined diameter from fabric.

Using a double thickness of sewing thread, baste around fabric circle 6" from edge. Place an even thickness of polyester fiberfill inside basting line. Center basket on fiberfill. Gently pull basting threads until fabric is gathered snugly around rim of basket; knot ends to secure. Turn edge of fabric to wrong side, tucking edge inside basting thread. Glue to rim of basket at basting line.

Centering design, trim stitched piece to measure 31¹/₂" x 4¹/₂".

Continued on page 73.

OLD-TIME SAMPLER

X	DMC	X	DMC
⊙	347	•	950
⊖	610	◉	3328
♡	612	◆	3362
−	676	✕	3363
+	677	□	3364
★	680	Grey area indicates last
▽	729	row of previous section
◇	760	of design.

Angel

Design #2

Design #3

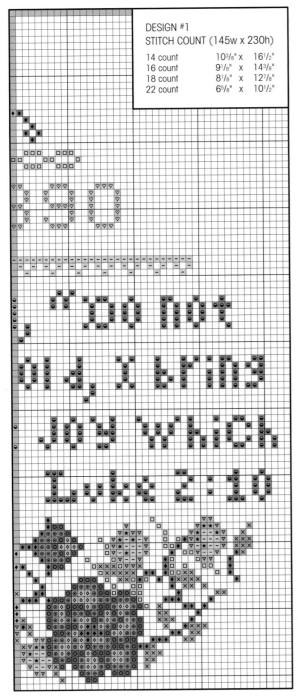

DESIGN #1		
STITCH COUNT (145w x 230h)		
14 count	10³/₈" x	16¹/₂"
16 count	9¹/₈" x	14³/₈"
18 count	8¹/₈" x	12⁷/₈"
22 count	6⁵/₈" x	10¹/₂"

Design #4

Matching right sides and long edges, fold stitched piece in half. Use a ¹/₂" seam allowance to sew long edges together; turn stitched piece right side out. With seam centered in back, press stitched piece flat. Press short edges ¹/₂" to wrong side.

Referring to photo, glue stitched piece around basket covering basting line.

Sampler Mini Stocking (shown on page 22): Design #5 was stitched over 2 fabric threads on a 12" x 6" piece of Cream Belfast Linen (32 ct). Two strands of floss were used for Cross Stitch. Personalize stocking cuff using DMC 347 floss and upper case alphabet from chart.

For stocking, you will need a 9" x 3¹/₄" piece of fabric for cuff backing, two 7" x 9" pieces of fabric for stocking, 6" length of ¹/₄"w ribbon for hanger, tracing paper, pencil, and fabric marking pencil.

Centering design, trim stitched piece to measure 9" x 3¹/₄".

Trace pattern onto tracing paper; add a ¹/₂" seam allowance on all sides and cut out pattern. Matching right sides and raw edges, place stocking fabric pieces together; place pattern on fabric pieces and pin pattern in place. Use fabric marking pencil to draw around pattern; remove pattern and cut out on drawn line. Matching right sides and leaving top open, use a ¹/₂" seam allowance to sew stocking pieces together. Clip seam allowance at curves and turn stocking right side out.

For stocking cuff, match right sides and short edges; fold stitched piece in half. Using a ¹/₂" seam allowance, sew short edges together. Repeat for cuff backing. Matching right sides, raw edges, and seams, use a ¹/₂" seam allowance to sew cuff and cuff backing together along lower edge of cuff; turn right side out and press. Baste cuff and cuff backing together close to raw edges.

Referring to photo and matching raw edges, place right side of cuff to inside of stocking with cuff back seam at center back of stocking. Use a ¹/₂" seam allowance to sew cuff and stocking together. Fold cuff 2¹/₄" to outside of stocking and press.

For hanger, fold ribbon in half, matching short edges. Referring to photo, blind stitch to inside of stocking.

Old-Time Sampler Ornaments (shown on page 25): Designs #2, #3, #4, and the angel only from Design #1 were each stitched over 2 fabric threads on a 7" x 5" piece of Cream Cashel Linen® (28 ct). Three strands of floss were used for Cross Stitch.

For each ornament, you will need a 6" x 4" piece of Cream Cashel Linen® for backing, 5" x 8" piece of adhesive mounting board, tracing paper, pencil, 5" x 8" piece of batting, 14" length of ¹/₄" dia. purchased cording with attached seam allowance, 6" length of ³/₈"w ribbon for hanger, 8" length of ³/₈"w ribbon for bow, and clear-drying craft glue.

For pattern, fold tracing paper in half and place fold on dashed line of desired pattern; trace pattern onto tracing paper. Cut out pattern; unfold and press flat. Draw around pattern twice on mounting board and twice on batting; cut out. Remove paper from one piece of mounting board and press one batting piece onto mounting board. Repeat with remaining mounting board and batting.

Referring to photo, position pattern on wrong side of stitched piece; pin pattern in place. Cut stitched piece 1" larger than pattern on all sides. Cut backing fabric same size as stitched piece. Clip ¹/₂" into edge of stitched piece at ¹/₂" intervals. Center wrong side of stitched piece over batting on one mounting board piece; fold edges of stitched piece to back of mounting board and glue in place. For ornament back, repeat with backing fabric and remaining mounting board.

Beginning and ending at top center of stitched piece, glue cording seam allowance to wrong side of ornament front, overlapping ends of cording.

For hanger, fold ribbon in half, matching short edges. Referring to photo, glue to wrong side of ornament front. Matching wrong sides, glue ornament front and back together. Tie 8" length of ribbon in a bow and, referring to photo, glue bow to ornament; trim ends as desired.

Designs by Linda Culp Calhoun.

BENEVOLENT GENT

Benevolent Gent Stocking
(shown on page 27): The design was stitched over 2 fabric threads on a 16" x 21" piece of Raw Cashel Linen® (28 ct). Three strands of floss were used for Cross Stitch and 1 strand for Backstitch. To complete stocking, see Finishing Instructions, page 92.

Benevolent Gent Bellpull
(shown on page 26): A portion of the design (refer to photo) was stitched over 2 fabric threads on a 16" x 20" piece of Raw Cashel Linen® (28 ct). Three strands of floss were used for Cross Stitch and 1 strand for Backstitch. To complete bellpull, see Finishing Instructions, page 92.

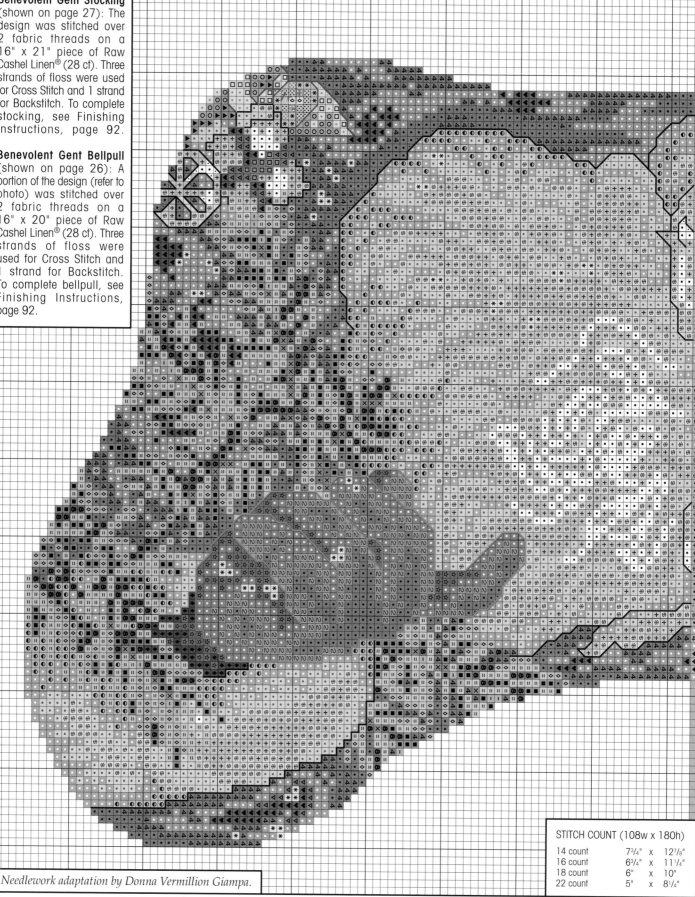

Needlework adaptation by Donna Vermillion Giampa.

STITCH COUNT (108w x 180h)		
14 count	7³/₄" x	12⁷/₈"
16 count	6³/₄" x	11¹/₄"
18 count	6" x	10"
22 count	5" x	8¹/₄"

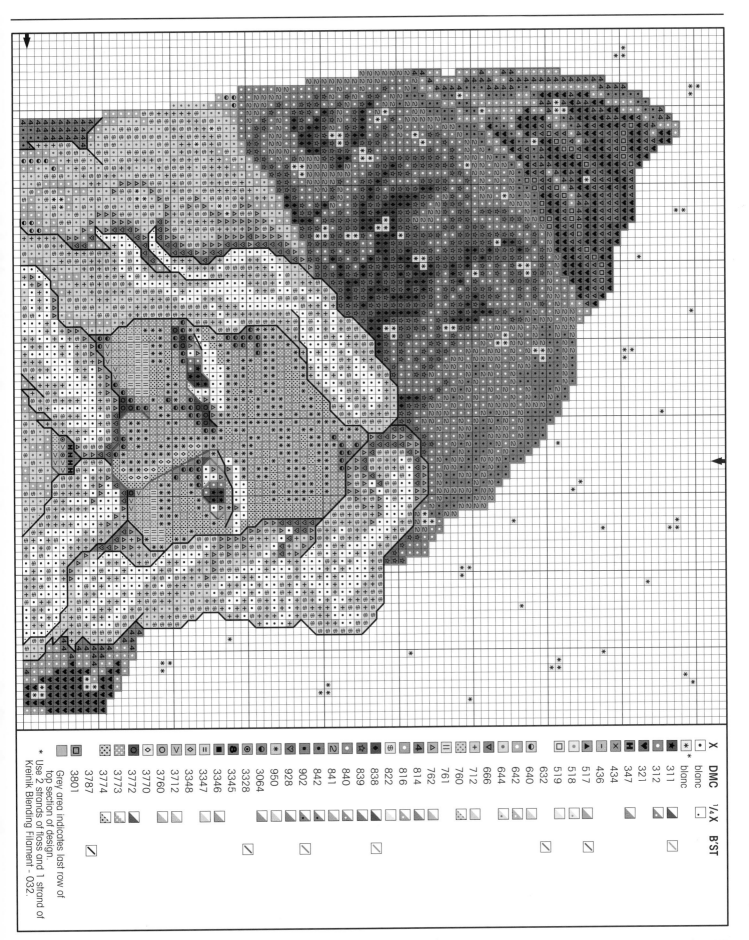

father christmas

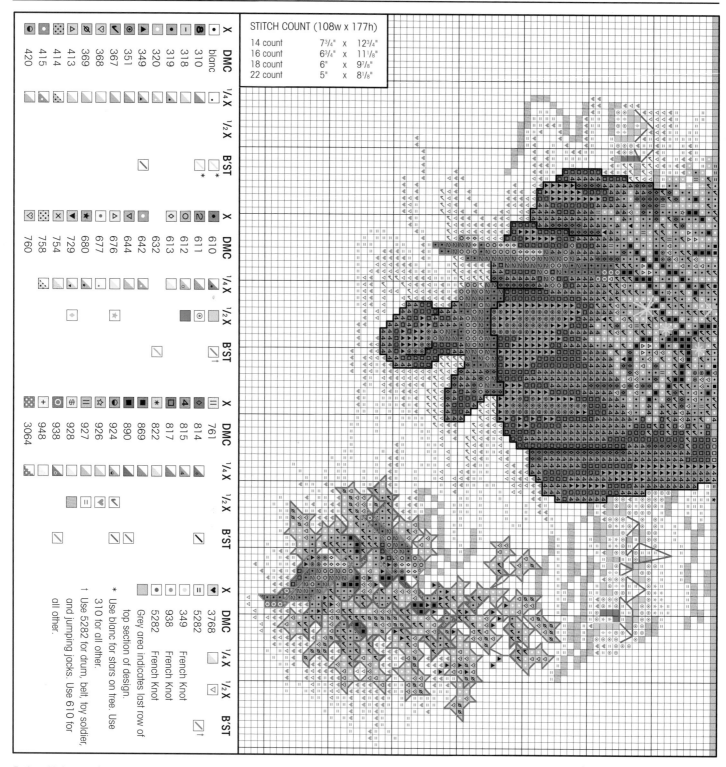

STITCH COUNT (108w x 177h)

14 count	7¾"	x	12¾"
16 count	6¾"	x	11⅛"
18 count	6"	x	9⅞"
22 count	5"	x	8⅛"

Color key (columns: X · ¼X · ½X · B'ST · DMC):

DMC
blanc
310
318
319
320
349
351
367
368
369
413
414
415
420

DMC
610
611
612
613
632
642
644
676
677
680
729
754
758
760

DMC
761
814
815
817
822
869
890
924
926
927
928
938
948
3064

DMC	
3768	French Knot
5282	French Knot
938	French Knot
349	French Knot
5282	

Grey area indicates last row of top section of design.

* Use blanc for stars on tree. Use 310 for all other.

† Use 5282 for drum, belt, toy soldier, and jumping jacks. Use 610 for all other.

Father Christmas Stocking (shown on page 29): The design was stitched over 2 fabric threads on a 16" x 21" piece of Spruce Green Cashel Linen® (28 ct). Three strands of floss were used for Cross Stitch and 1 strand for Half Cross Stitch, Backstitch, and French Knots. Personalize stocking using alphabet provided, page 89. To complete stocking, see Finishing Instructions, page 93.

Father Christmas Standing Figure (shown on page 28): A portion of the design (refer to photo) was stitched over 2 fabric threads on a 14" x 18" piece of Spruce Green Cashel Linen® (28 ct). Three strands of floss were used for Cross Stitch and 1 strand for Half Cross Stitch, Backstitch, and French Knots.

For standing figure, you will need a 9" x 14" piece of Cashel Linen® for backing, a 7" x 5" piece of Cashel Linen® for base, tracing paper, fabric marking pencil, small plastic bag, aquarium gravel, and polyester fiberfill.

Centering design, trim stitched piece to measure 9" x 14".

Matching right sides and raw edges and leaving bottom edge open, sew stitched piece and backing together ½" from design. Trim bottom edge of figure ¾" from bottom edge of design. Leaving a ¼" seam allowance, cut out figure. Clip seam allowances at curves; turn figure right side out and carefully push curves outward. Press raw edges at bottom edge ¼" to wrong side; stuff figure with polyester fiberfill to 1½" from opening.

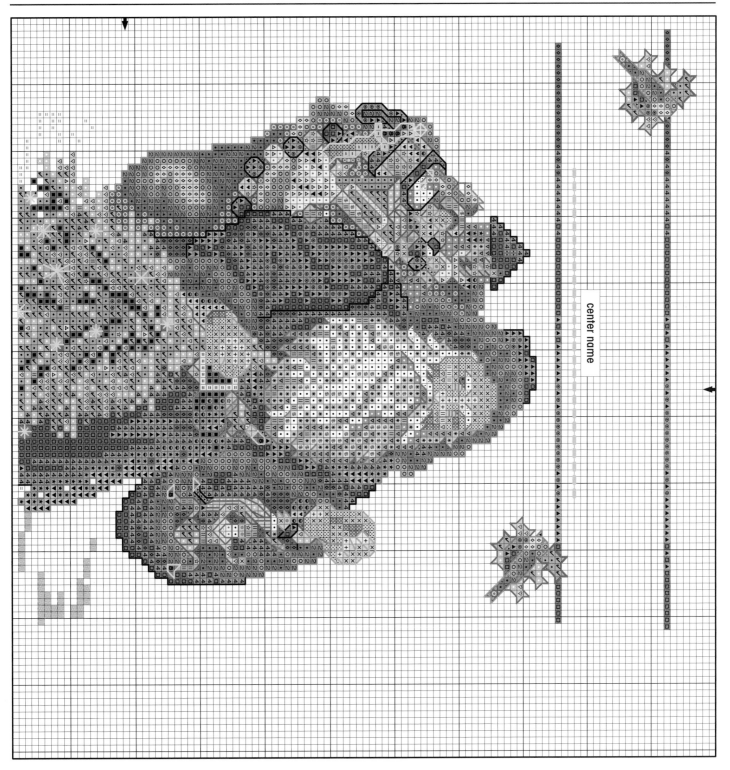

center name

For base, place figure on tracing paper and draw around figure. Add a
1/2" seam allowance to pattern; cut out. Place pattern on a piece of Cashel
Linen®. Use fabric marking pencil to draw around pattern; cut out along
drawn line. Baste around base piece 1/2" from raw edge; press raw edges
to wrong side along basting line.

To weight bottom of figure, fill a plastic bag with a small amount of
aquarium gravel. Insert bag of gravel into opening of figure.

Pin wrong side of base piece over opening. Whipstitch in place, adding
polyester fiberfill as necessary to fill bottom of figure. Remove basting thread.

Needlework adaptation by Donna Vermillion Giampa.

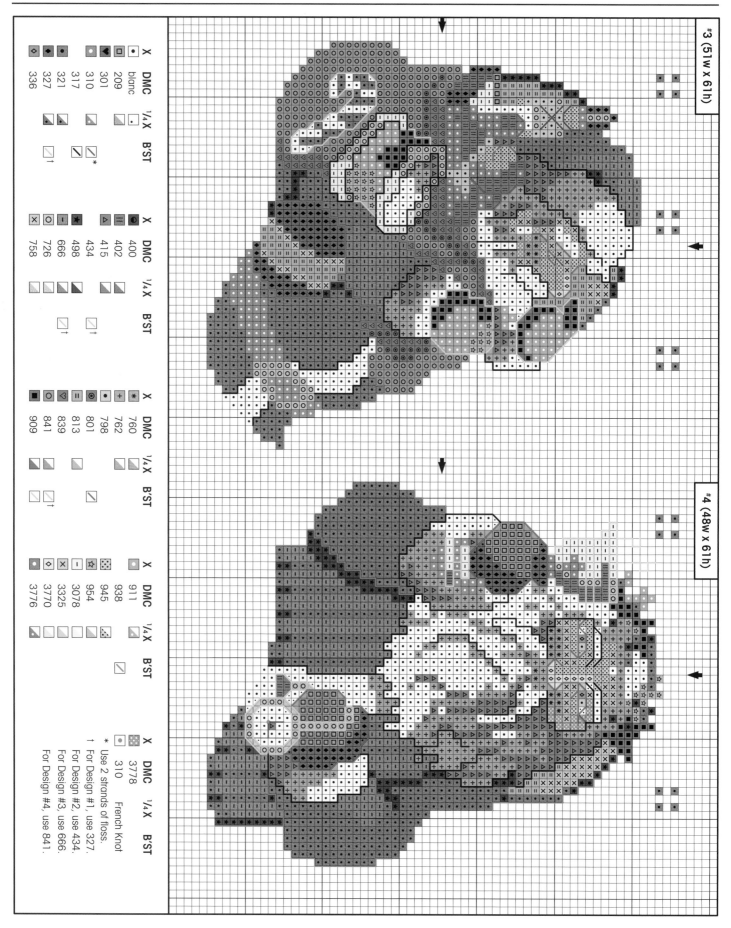

#3 (51w x 61h)

X	DMC	¼X	B'ST
◇	blanc		
◆	209		
▨	301	▨	
◐	310	▨	*
◀	317	▨	◹
□	321	▨	◹
·	327	▨	◹ †
	336		

X	DMC	¼X	B'ST
▷	400	▨	
▤	402		
◑	415		
×	434	▨	◹ †
◯	498	▨	◹ †
‖	666		
✱	726		
	758	▨	

X	DMC	¼X	B'ST
■	760	▨	
◯	762		
◁	798		
‖	801	▨	†
◉	813		
·	839		
+	841	▨	
✱	909		

#4 (48w x 61h)

X	DMC	¼X	B'ST
▨	911		
◇	938	▨	
×	945	▨	◹
‖	954		
▨	3078	▨	
▨	3325	▨	
▨	3770		
▨	3776	▨	

X	DMC	¼X	B'ST
▨	3778	▨	
·	310 French Knot		

* Use 2 strands of floss.
† For Design #1, use 327.
† For Design #2, use 434.
† For Design #3, use 666.
† For Design #4, use 841.

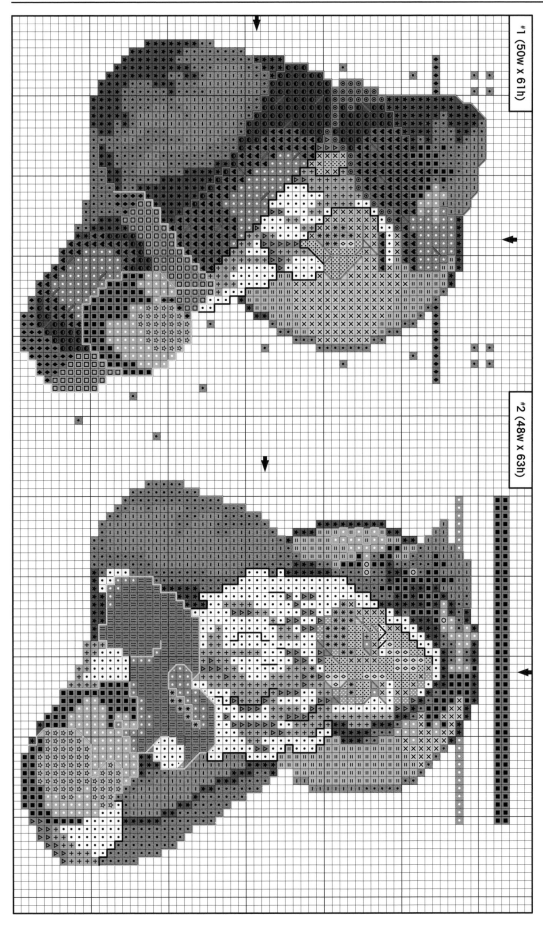

#1 (50w x 61h)

#2 (48w x 63h)

Santas Around the World Stockings
(shown on page 31): Each design was stitched on a 9" square of Antique White Aida (14 ct). Three strands of floss were used for Cross Stitch and 1 strand for Half Cross Stitch, Backstitch, and French Knot.

For each ornament, you will need a 9" square piece of fabric for backing, 2" x 15" bias fabric strip for cording, 15" length of ¹/₈" dia. purchased cord, tracing paper, pencil, fabric marking pencil, and 6" length of ¹/₄"w ribbon for hanger.

For pattern, trace Stocking Pattern, page 95, onto tracing paper; cut out pattern. Referring to photo, position pattern on wrong side of stitched piece; pin pattern in place. Use fabric marking pencil to draw around pattern; remove pattern and cut out on drawn line. Use pattern and cut one from backing fabric.

For cording, center cord on wrong side of bias strip; matching long edges, fold strip over cord. Use a zipper foot to baste along length of strip close to cord; trim seam allowance to ¹/₂". Matching raw edges, baste cording to right side of stocking front. Trim away excess cording.

Matching right sides and leaving top edge open, use a ¹/₂" seam allowance to sew stitched piece and backing fabric together. Turn top edge of stocking ¹/₂" to wrong side and hem. Clip seam allowance at curves and turn stocking right side out.

For hanger, fold ribbon in half and blind stitch to inside of stocking at left seam.

Mini Stocking Wreath (shown on page 30): Each design was stitched on a 9" square of Antique White Aida (14 ct). Three strands of floss were used for Cross Stitch and 1 strand for Half Cross Stitch, Backstitch, and French Knot. Refer to Santas Around the World Stockings instructions above to make stockings. They were attached to an 18" dia. decorated wreath.

*Designs by
Kooler Design Studio.*

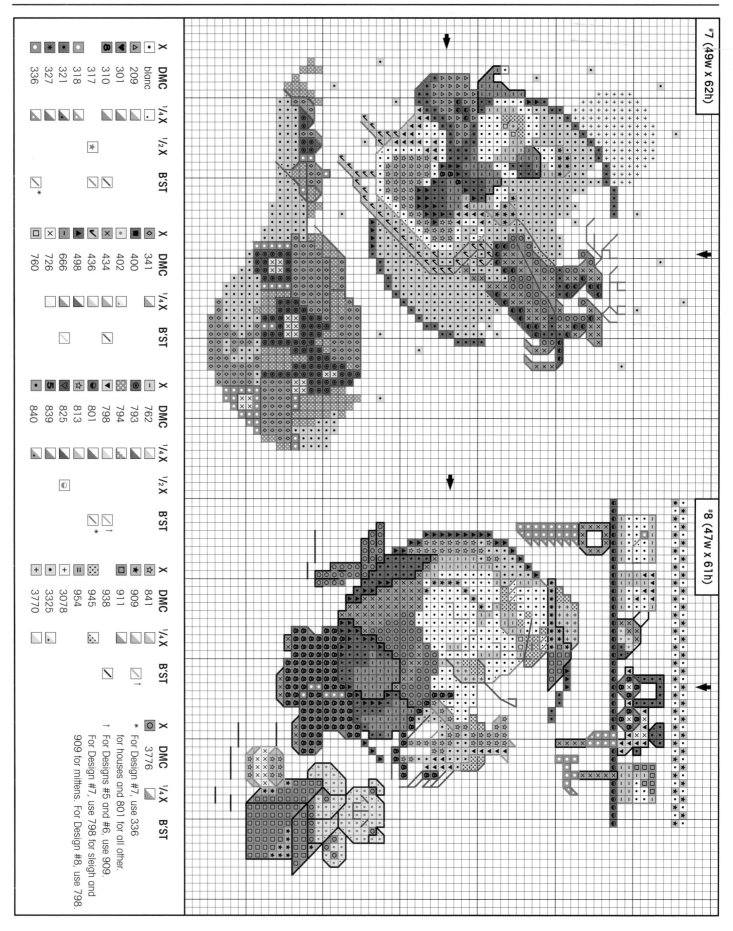

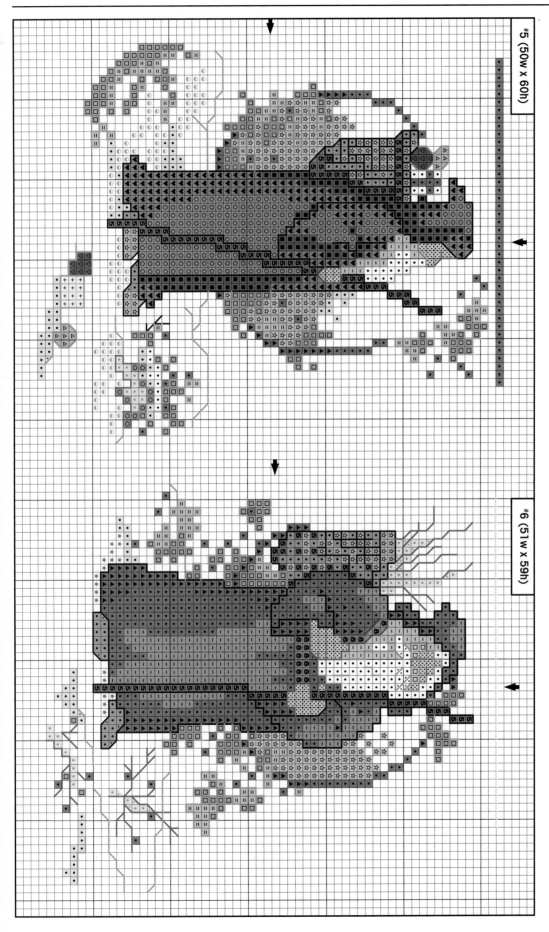

Santas Around the World Stockings

(shown on page 31): Each design was stitched on a 9" square of Antique White Aida (14 ct). Three strands of floss were used for Cross Stitch and 1 strand for Half Cross Stitch, Backstitch, and French Knot.

For each ornament, you will need a 9" square piece of fabric for backing, 2" x 15" bias fabric strip for cording, 15" length of ⅛" dia. purchased cord, tracing paper, pencil, fabric marking pencil, and 6" length of ¼"w ribbon for hanger.

For pattern, trace Stocking Pattern, page 95, onto tracing paper; cut out pattern. Referring to photo, position pattern on wrong side of stitched piece; pin pattern in place. Use fabric marking pencil to draw around pattern; remove pattern and cut out on drawn line. Use pattern and cut one from backing fabric.

For cording, center cord on wrong side of bias strip; matching long edges, fold strip over cord. Use a zipper foot to baste along length of strip close to cord; trim seam allowance to ½". Matching raw edges, baste cording to right side of stocking front. Trim away excess cording.

Matching right sides and leaving top edge open, use a ½" seam allowance to sew stitched piece and backing fabric together. Turn top edge of stocking ½" to wrong side and hem. Clip seam allowance at curves and turn stocking right side out.

For hanger, fold ribbon in half and blind stitch to inside of stocking at left seam.

Mini Stocking Wreath (shown on page 30): Each design was stitched on a 9" square of Antique White Aida (14 ct). Three strands of floss were used for Cross Stitch and 1 strand for Half Cross Stitch, Backstitch, and French Knot. Refer to Santas Around the World Stockings instructions above to make stockings. They were attached to an 18" dia. decorated wreath.

Designs by
Kooler Design Studio.

childhood pleasures

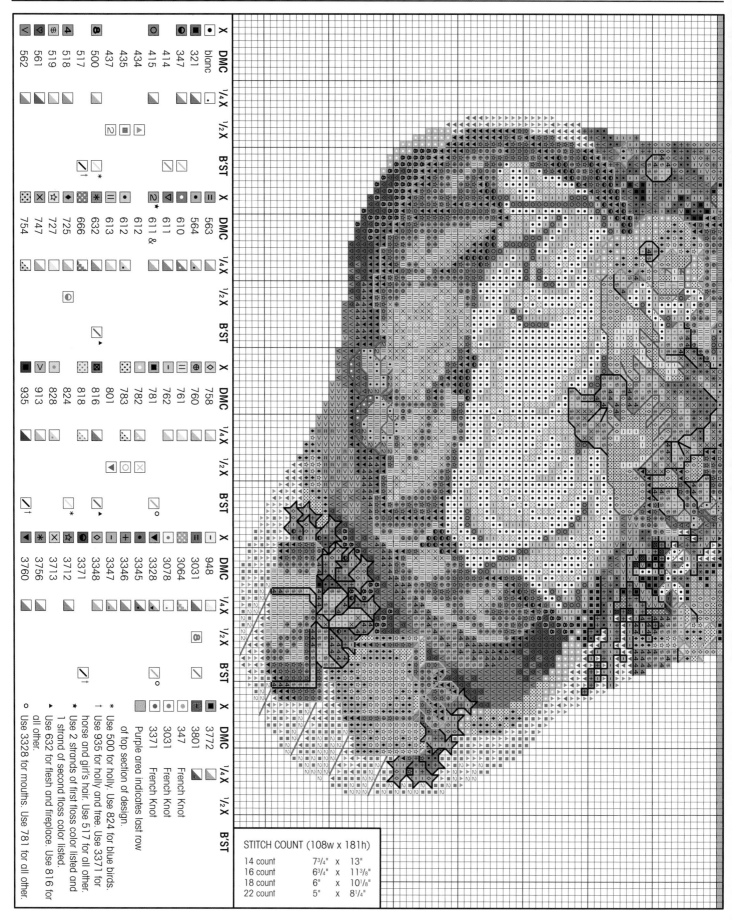

X							DMC	1/4X	1/2X	B'ST
◁	◀	⊞	▲	◙	○	◐■	blanc			
							321			
							347			
							414			
							415			
			2	■	▶		434			
							435			
		◣	□				437			
				✳			500			
							517			
							518			
							519			
							561			
							562			

X							DMC	1/4X	1/2X	B'ST
⊡	✕	☆	◆	⊠	✳	•	563			
				‖	•	‖	564			
			2*	◀	•	•	610			
							611 &			
							611			
							612		◐	
							612			
							613			▶
							632			
							666			
							725			
							727			
							747			
							754			

X							DMC	1/4X	1/2X	B'ST
■	✓	⊠		▨	○	◐	758			
			■	‖	⊞	◇	760			
							761		◀	
							762		○	
							781		✕	
							782			
							783			°
							801			
							816			
							818			
							824			
							828			
							913			
							935			

X							DMC	1/4X	1/2X	B'ST
◀	✳	✕	☆	◐	◇	‖	948		⊞	
					‖	‖	3031			
							3064			
							3078			
							3328			
							3345			
							3346			
							3347			
							3348			
							3371			
							3712			
							3713			
							3756			
							3760			

X					DMC	1/4X	1/2X	B'ST
▨	•	●	•	■	3772			
					3801			
					347	French Knot
					3031	French Knot
					3371	French Knot

Purple area indicates last row of top section of design.

* Use 500 for holly. Use 824 for blue birds.

† Use 935 for holly and tree. Use 517 for all other.

◇ Use 2 strands of first floss color listed and 1 strand of second floss color listed.

▶ Use 632 for flesh and fireplace. Use 816 for all other.

° Use 3328 for mouths. Use 781 for all other.

STITCH COUNT (108w x 181h)

14 count	7³/₄"	x	13"
16 count	6³/₄"	x	11³/₈"
18 count	6"	x	10¹/₈"
22 count	5"	x	8¹/₄"

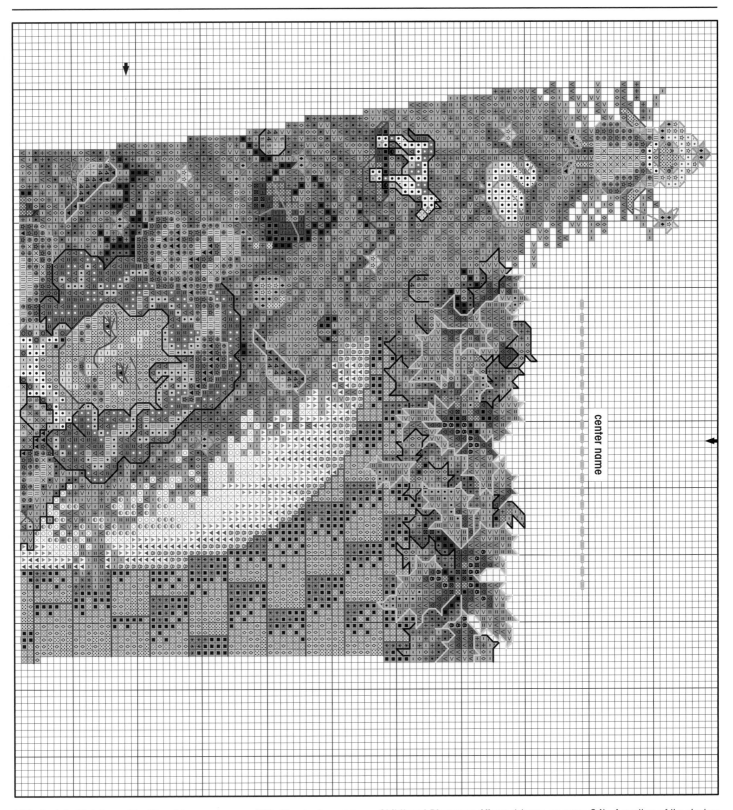

center name

Little Lady's Christmas Stocking (shown on page 36): The design was stitched over 2 fabric threads on a 16" x 21" piece of Antique White Cashel Linen® (28 ct). Three strands of floss were used for Cross Stitch and 1 strand for Half Cross Stitch, Backstitch, and French Knots. Personalize stocking using alphabet provided, page 87. To complete stocking, see Finishing Instructions, page 93.

Childhood Pleasures Album (shown on page 34): A portion of the design (refer to photo) was stitched over 2 fabric threads on a 14" x 15" piece of Tile Blue Linda® (27 ct). Three strands of floss were used for Cross Stitch and 1 strand for Half Cross Stitch and Backstitch. To complete album, see Finishing Instructions, page 87.

Needlework adaptation by Donna Vermillion Giampa.

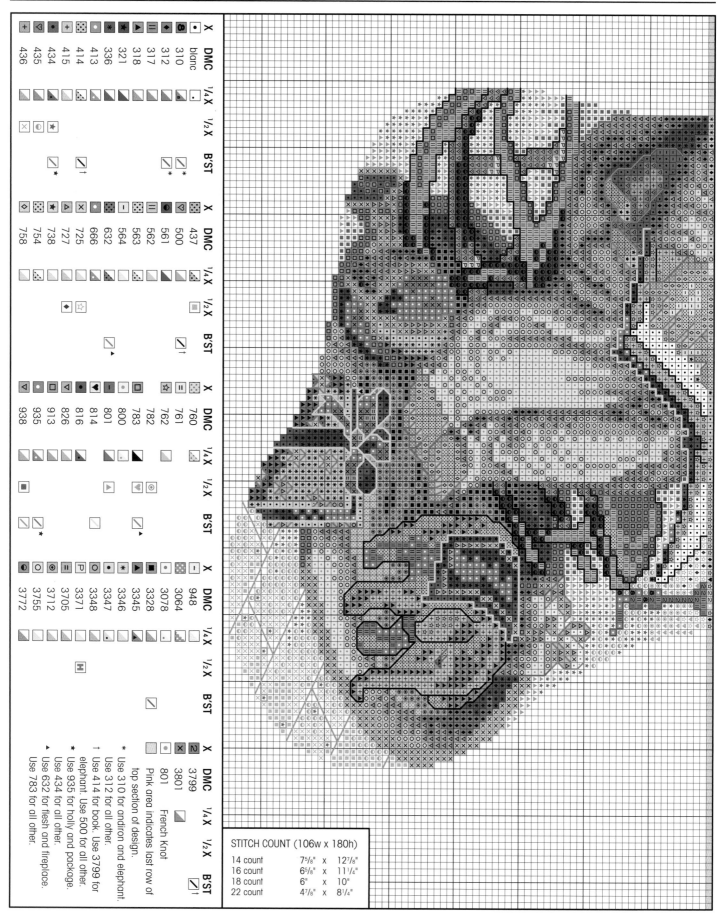

X	DMC	¼X	½X	B'ST
	blanc			
	310		×	
	312		◐	
	317		★	
	318			
	321			
	336			
	413			
	414			↑
	415			
	434			*
	435			
	436			

X	DMC	¼X	½X	B'ST
	437			
	500			
	561			
	562			
	563		■	
	564			
	632			
	666		◆	↑
	725		☆	
	727			▶
	738			
	754			
	758			

X	DMC	¼X	½X	B'ST
	760			
	761			↑
	762			
	782		▶	
	783		◀	
	800		◉	
	801			
	814		■	
	816			
	826		▶	
	913		◀	
	935		◉	▶
	938			

X	DMC	¼X	½X	B'ST
	948			
	3064			
	3078			
	3328			
	3345			
	3346			
	3347			
	3348			
	3371			
	3705			
	3712		▶	
	3755		◀	
	3772			

X		DMC	¼X	½X	B'ST
		3799			
×	2	3801			↑
●		801	French Knot		

Pink area indicates last row of top section of design.

* Use 310 for andiron and elephant. Use 312 for all other.
↑ Use 414 for book. Use 3799 for elephant. Use 500 for all other.
★ Use 935 for holly and package. Use 434 for all other.
▶ Use 632 for flesh and fireplace. Use 783 for all other.

STITCH COUNT (106w x 180h)

14 count	7⅝"	x	12⅞"
16 count	6⅝"	x	11¼"
18 count	6"	x	10"
22 count	4⅞"	x	8¼"

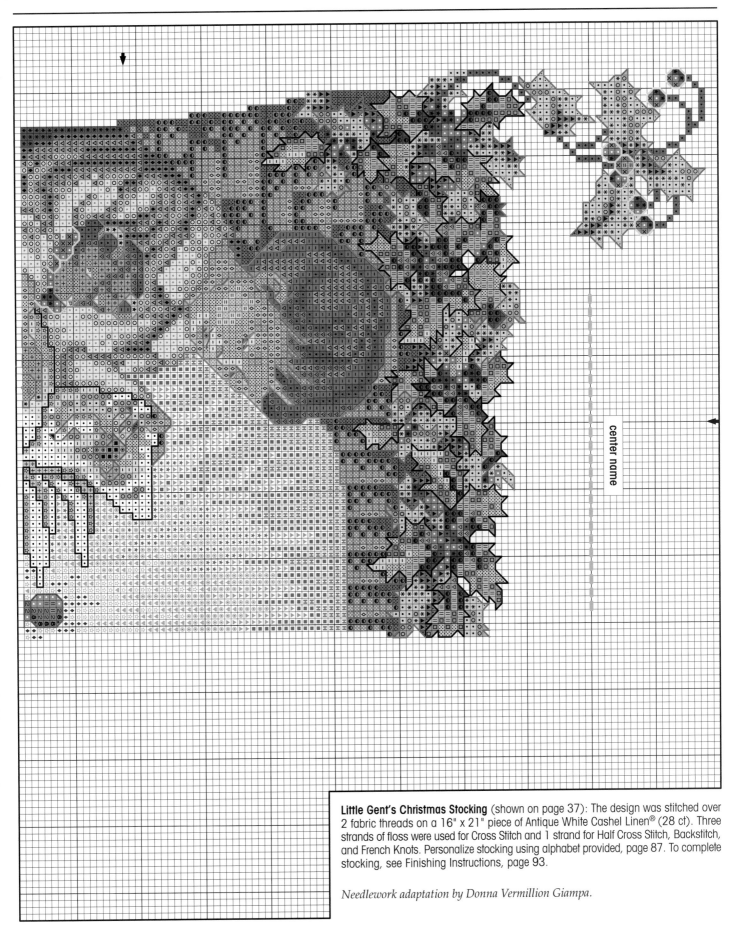

center name

Little Gent's Christmas Stocking (shown on page 37): The design was stitched over 2 fabric threads on a 16" x 21" piece of Antique White Cashel Linen® (28 ct). Three strands of floss were used for Cross Stitch and 1 strand for Half Cross Stitch, Backstitch, and French Knots. Personalize stocking using alphabet provided, page 87. To complete stocking, see Finishing Instructions, page 93.

Needlework adaptation by Donna Vermillion Giampa.

childhood pleasures

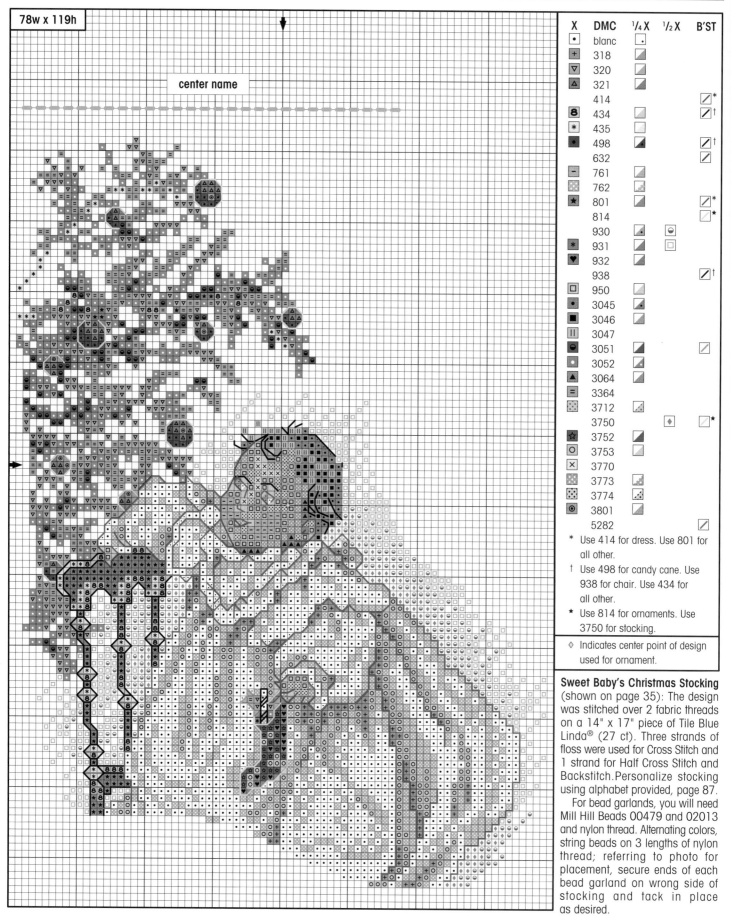

78w x 119h

center name

X	DMC	¼X	½X	B'ST
•	blanc	•		
+	318			
▽	320			
▲	321			
	414			⟋*
8	434			⟋†
*	435			
●	498			⟋†
	632			⟋
–	761			
▦	762			
★	801			⟋*
	814			⟋*
	930		◉	
*	931		□	
♥	932			
	938			⟋†
▢	950			
●	3045			
■	3046			
‖	3047			
●	3051			⟋
	3052			
▲	3064			
=	3364			
▦	3712			
	3750		◆	⟋*
☆	3752			
○	3753			
✕	3770			
▦	3773			
▦	3774			
◉	3801			
	5282			⟋

* Use 414 for dress. Use 801 for all other.

† Use 498 for candy cane. Use 938 for chair. Use 434 for all other.

★ Use 814 for ornaments. Use 3750 for stocking.

◇ Indicates center point of design used for ornament.

Sweet Baby's Christmas Stocking (shown on page 35): The design was stitched over 2 fabric threads on a 14" x 17" piece of Tile Blue Linda® (27 ct). Three strands of floss were used for Cross Stitch and 1 strand for Half Cross Stitch and Backstitch. Personalize stocking using alphabet provided, page 87.

For bead garlands, you will need Mill Hill Beads 00479 and 02013 and nylon thread. Alternating colors, string beads on 3 lengths of nylon thread; referring to photo for placement, secure ends of each bead garland on wrong side of stocking and tack in place as desired.

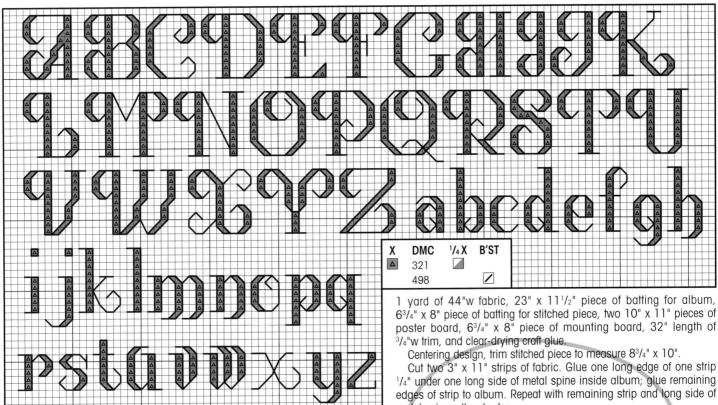

X	DMC	¹/₄ X	B'ST
▲	321	◢	
	498		◿

For stocking, you will need an 8" x 14" piece of fabric for backing, two 8" x 14" pieces of fabric for lining, 29" length of ¹/₄" dia. purchased cording with attached seam allowance, 10¹/₂" length of 1⁵/₈"w lace, 2" x 5" piece of fabric for hanger, tracing paper, and fabric marking pencil.

For stocking pattern, match arrows to form one pattern and trace pattern onto tracing paper; add a ¹/₂" seam allowance on all sides and cut out pattern. Referring to photo for placement, position pattern on wrong side of stitched piece; pin pattern in place. Use fabric marking pencil to draw around pattern; remove pattern and cut out on drawn line. Use pattern and cut **one** from backing fabric and **two** from lining fabric.

If needed, trim seam allowance of cording to ¹/₂". Matching raw edges, baste cording to right side of stocking front.

Matching right sides and leaving top edge open, use a ¹/₂" seam allowance to sew stitched piece and backing fabric together. Clip seam allowance at curves and turn stocking right side out. Press top edge of stocking ¹/₂" to wrong side.

Matching right sides and leaving top edge open, use a ⁵/₈" seam allowance to sew lining pieces together; trim seam allowance close to stitching. **Do not turn lining right side out.** Press top edge of lining ¹/₂" to wrong side.

For hanger, press each long edge of fabric strip ¹/₂" to center. Matching long edges, fold strip in half and sew close to folded edges. Matching short edges, fold hanger in half and whipstitch to inside of stocking at left seam. With wrong sides facing, place lining inside stocking; blind stitch lining to stocking.

For cuff, press short edges of lace ¹/₂" to wrong side. Referring to photo, pin lace around top edge of stocking and blind stitch lace in place.

Baby Ornament (shown on page 35): A portion of the design was stitched over 2 fabric threads on a 5" square of Antique White Cashel Linen® (28 ct). Three strands of floss were used for Cross Stitch and 1 strand for Half Cross Stitch and Backstitch. It was inserted in a purchased gold round frame (2¹/₂" dia. opening). Matching center of frame opening to center of design (indicated by ◇ on chart), stitch area of design required to fill frame opening.

FINISHING INSTRUCTIONS
Childhood Pleasures Album (shown on page 34, chart on pages 82-83).
For album, you will need a 10¹/₂" x 11¹/₂" photo album with a 2¹/₄" spine,

1 yard of 44"w fabric, 23" x 11¹/₂" piece of batting for album, 6³/₄" x 8" piece of batting for stitched piece, two 10" x 11" pieces of poster board, 6³/₄" x 8" piece of mounting board, 32" length of ³/₄"w trim, and clear-drying craft glue.

Centering design, trim stitched piece to measure 8³/₄" x 10".

Cut two 3" x 11" strips of fabric. Glue one long edge of one strip ¹/₄" under one long side of metal spine inside album; glue remaining edges of strip to album. Repeat with remaining strip and long side of metal spine; allow to dry.

Glue batting to outside of album. Cut a 25" x 13¹/₂" piece of fabric for outside of album. Center album, batting side down, on wrong side of fabric; fold fabric at corners to inside of album and glue in place. At center bottom of album, turn a 4" section of fabric ¹/₄" to wrong side (**Fig. 1**); glue folded edge under spine of album. Repeat at center top of album. Fold remaining edges of fabric to inside of album and glue in place; allow to dry.

Fig. 1

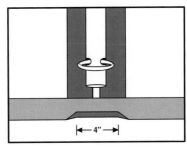

Cut two 12" x 13" pieces of fabric for inside covers. Center one piece of poster board on wrong side of one piece of fabric; fold edges of fabric to back of poster board and glue in place. Glue wrong side of covered poster board to inside of front cover of album approximately ¹/₄" from top, bottom, and outside edges of album. Repeat with remaining piece of fabric and poster board for inside back cover.

To mount stitched piece, glue batting to mounting board. Center stitched piece on batting and fold edges of stitched piece to back of mounting board; glue in place. Center and glue wrong side of mounted stitched piece to front cover.

Beginning at lower right corner of stitched piece, glue trim around outside edge of stitched piece; trim ends.

Needlework adaptation by Donna Vermillion Giampa.

BOTANICAL BEAUTIES

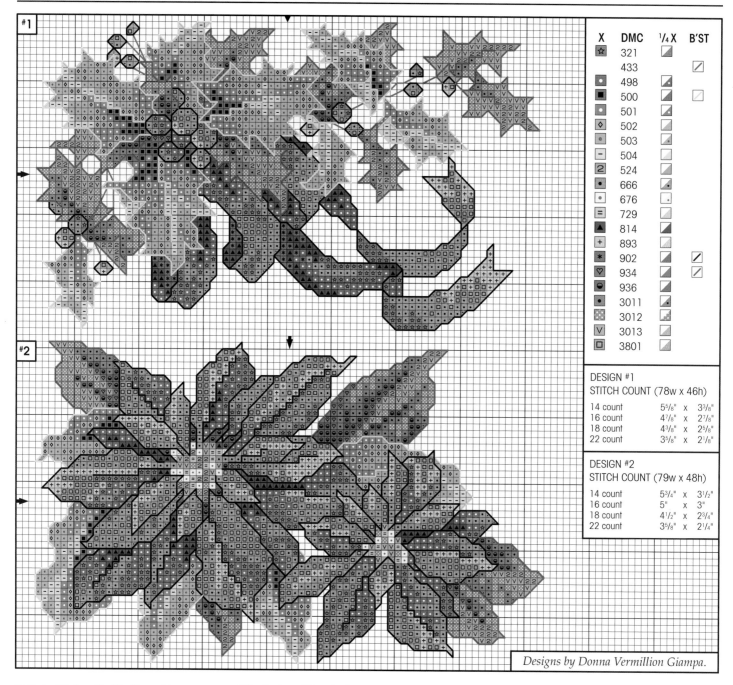

X	DMC	¼ X	B'ST
☆	321	◩	
	433		◪
◉	498	◩	
■	500	◩	◪
▣	501	◩	
◇	502	◩	
◔	503	◩	
−	504	◩	
2	524	◩	
◆	666	◩	
◦	676	◌	
=	729	◩	
▲	814	◩	
+	893	◩	
✳	902	◩	◪
♡	934	◩	◪
◒	936	◩	
◉	3011	◪	
▨	3012	◪	
V	3013	◩	
▢	3801	◩	

DESIGN #1
STITCH COUNT (78w x 46h)

14 count	5⅝"	x	3⅜"
16 count	4⅞"	x	2⅞"
18 count	4⅜"	x	2⅝"
22 count	3⅝"	x	2⅛"

DESIGN #2
STITCH COUNT (79w x 48h)

14 count	5¾"	x	3½"
16 count	5"	x	3"
18 count	4½"	x	2¾"
22 count	3⅝"	x	2¼"

Designs by Donna Vermillion Giampa.

Holly and Poinsettia Stockings (shown on page 33): Designs #1 and #2 were each stitched over 2 fabric threads on a 15" x 10" piece of Cream Cashel Linen® (28 ct). Three strands of floss were used for Cross Stitch and 1 strand for Backstitch.

For each stocking, you will need a 14½" x 6½" piece of fabric for cuff backing, 18" length of ¼" dia. purchased cording with attached seam allowance, two 8" x 16" pieces of fabric for stocking, two 8" x 16" pieces of fabric for lining, 2" x 6" piece of fabric for hanger, tracing paper, and fabric marking pencil.

Centering design horizontally with top of design 2" from one long edge of fabric, trim stitched piece to measure 14½" x 6½".

For stocking cuff, match right sides and short edges; fold stitched piece in half. Using a ½" seam allowance, sew short edges together. Repeat for cuff backing.

If needed, trim seam allowance of cording to ½". Matching raw edges and beginning at back seam, pin cording to lower edge of right side of stitched piece. Ends of cording should overlap approximately 4". Turn

overlapped ends of cording toward outside of stitched piece; baste cording to stitched piece.

Matching right sides, raw edges, and seams, use a ½" seam allowance to sew cuff and cuff backing together along lower edge of cuff; turn right side out and press. Baste cuff and cuff backing together close to raw edges.

For stocking pattern, match arrows of Stocking Pattern, page 92, to form one pattern and trace pattern onto tracing paper; add a ½" seam allowance on all sides and cut out pattern. Matching right sides and raw edges, place stocking fabric pieces together; place pattern on fabric pieces and pin pattern in place. Use fabric marking pencil to draw around pattern; remove pattern and cut out on drawn line. Repeat with lining fabric pieces.

Matching right sides and leaving top edge open, use a ½" seam allowance to sew stocking pieces together. Clip seam allowance at curves and turn stocking right side out.

Matching right sides and leaving top edge open, use a ⅝" seam allowance to sew lining pieces together; trim seam allowance close to

Father Christmas Stocking (shown on page 29, chart on pages 76-77).

X	DMC
▲	349
⊙	351
◇	814
4	815
□	817

stitching. **Do not turn lining right side out.** With wrong sides facing, place lining inside stocking. Baste stocking and lining together close to raw edges.

Referring to photo and matching raw edges, match right side of cuff to inside of stocking with cuff back seam at center back of stocking. Use a 1/2" seam allowance to sew cuff and stocking together. Fold cuff 5" to outside of stocking and press.

For hanger, press each long edge of fabric strip 1/2" to center. Matching long edges, fold strip in half and sew close to folded edges. Fold hanger in half, matching short edges; refer to photo and blind stitch to inside of stocking.

Poinsettia Shaker Box (shown on page 32): Design #2 was stitched over 2 fabric threads on a 12" x 10" piece of Cream Cashel Linen® (28 ct). Three strands of floss were used for Cross Stitch and 1 strand for Backstitch.

For Shaker box you will need a 5 3/4" x 7" oval Shaker box, 5 3/4" x 7" oval piece of batting for lid, 3 1/2" x 21 1/2" piece of fabric for box bottom, 21" length of 1"w ribbon, tracing paper, pencil, fabric marking pencil, and clear-drying craft glue.

For pattern, trace around box lid onto tracing paper; add 3/4" on all sides and cut out. Center pattern on wrong side of stitched piece; pin pattern in place. Use a fabric marking pencil to draw around pattern; remove pattern and cut out on drawn line. Clip 1/4" into edge of stitched piece at 1" intervals. Glue batting on top of lid. Centering wrong side of stitched piece on batting, fold edges of stitched piece down and glue to side of lid. Referring to photo, glue ribbon to side of lid.

For box bottom, press fabric piece under 1/2" on short edges and 1/4" on one long edge. Placing folded edge along bottom edge of box, glue fabric to box. Fold top edge of fabric to inside of box and glue in place.

MR. SNOWMAN AND FRIENDS

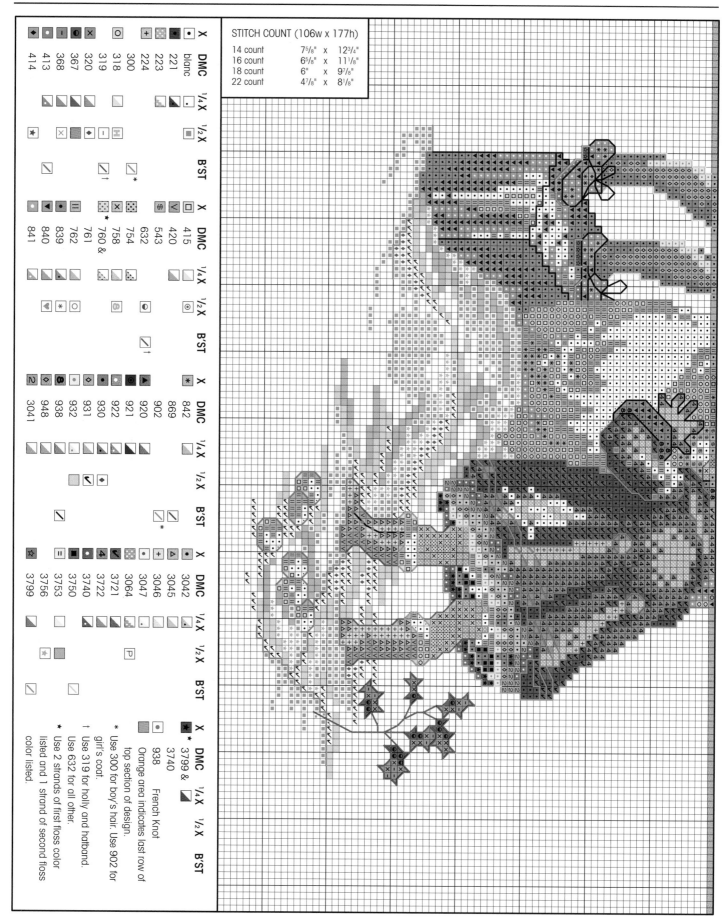

STITCH COUNT (106w x 177h)

14 count	7 5/8"	x	12 3/4"
16 count	6 5/8"	x	11 1/8"
18 count	6"	x	9 7/8"
22 count	4 7/8"	x	8 1/8"

* Orange area indicates last row of top section of design.
* Use 300 for boy's hair. Use 902 for girl's coat.
† Use 319 for holly and hatband.
‡ Use 632 for all other.
✱ Use 2 strands of first floss color listed and 1 strand of second floss color listed.

French Knot

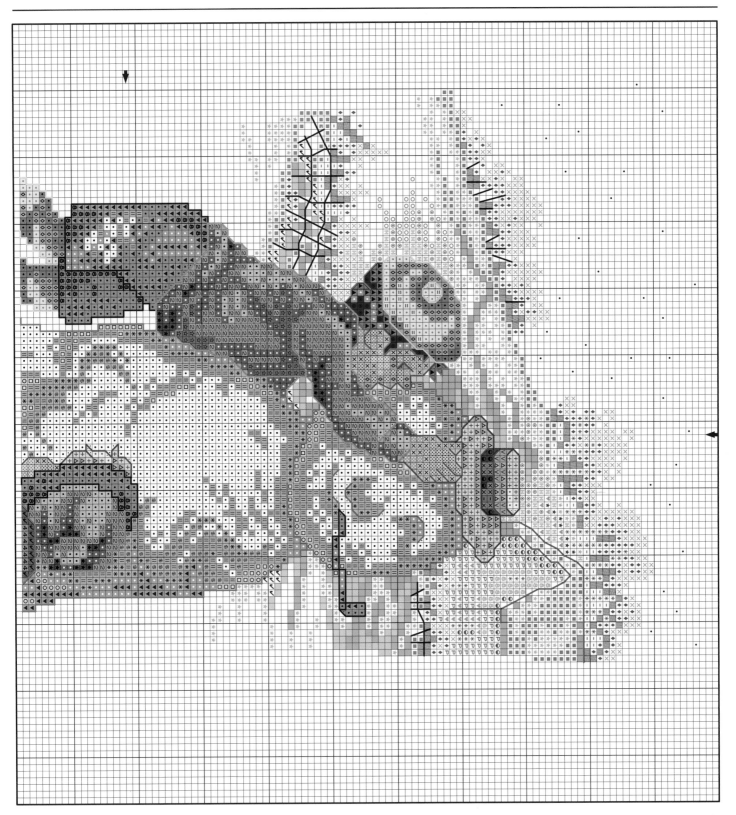

Mr. Snowman and Friends Stocking (shown on page 39): The design was stitched over 2 fabric threads on a 16" x 21" piece of Misty Blue Cashel Linen® (28 ct). Three strands of floss were used for Cross Stitch, 1 strand for Half Cross Stitch and Backstitch, and 2 strands for French Knots. To complete stocking, see Finishing Instructions, page 93.

Winter Fun Stocking (shown on page 38): A portion of the design (refer to photo) was stitched over 2 fabric threads on a 14" x 13" piece of Misty Blue Cashel Linen® (28 ct). Three strands of floss were used for Cross Stitch and 1 strand for Half Cross Stitch and Backstitch. To complete stocking, see Finishing Instructions, page 93.

Needlework adaptation by Donna Vermillion Giampa.

BENEVOLENT GENT

FINISHING INSTRUCTIONS

Benevolent Gent Stocking (shown on page 27, chart on pages 74-75): You will need an 8" x 16" piece of fabric for backing, two 8" x 16" pieces of fabric for lining, 37" length of $\frac{1}{4}$" dia. purchased cording with attached seam allowance, 13" x 5" piece of fur for cuff, 2" x 6" piece of fabric for hanger, tracing paper, and fabric marking pencil.

For stocking pattern, match arrows to form one pattern and trace pattern onto tracing paper; add a $\frac{1}{2}$" seam allowance on all sides and cut out pattern. Referring to photo for placement, position pattern on wrong side of stitched piece; pin pattern in place. Use fabric marking pencil to draw around pattern; remove pattern and cut out on drawn line. Use pattern and cut **one** from backing fabric and **two** from lining fabric.

If needed, trim seam allowance of cording to $\frac{1}{2}$". Matching raw edges, baste cording to right side of stocking front.

Matching right sides and leaving top edge open, use a $\frac{1}{2}$" seam allowance to sew stitched piece and backing fabric together. Clip seam allowance at curves and turn stocking right side out. Press top edge of stocking $\frac{1}{2}$" to wrong side.

Matching right sides and leaving top edge open, use a $\frac{5}{8}$" seam allowance to sew lining pieces together; trim seam allowance close to stitching. **Do not turn lining right side out.** Press top edge of lining $\frac{1}{2}$" to wrong side. With wrong sides facing, place lining inside stocking; blind stitch lining to stocking.

For cuff, beginning and ending at center back and overlapping short edges, position fur piece at top edge of stocking; blind stitch cuff in place.

For hanger, press each long edge of fabric strip $\frac{1}{2}$" to center. Matching long edges, fold strip in half and sew close to folded edges. Matching short edges, fold hanger in half and whipstitch to inside of stocking at left seam.

Benevolent Gent Bellpull (shown on page 26, chart on pages 74-75): You will need a 6$\frac{1}{4}$" x 15$\frac{1}{4}$" piece of fabric for backing, two 2" x 15$\frac{1}{4}$" lengths of bias fabric strip for cording, two 15$\frac{1}{4}$" lengths of $\frac{1}{4}$" dia. purchased cord, and bellpull hardware.

Centering design, trim stitched piece to measure 6$\frac{1}{4}$" x 15$\frac{1}{4}$".

For cording, center cord on wrong side of bias strip; matching long edges, fold strip over cord. Use a zipper foot to baste along length of strip close to cord; trim seam allowance to $\frac{1}{2}$". Matching long sides and raw edges, baste cording to right side of stitched piece.

Matching right sides and raw edges and leaving top and bottom edges open, use a $\frac{1}{2}$" seam allowance to sew backing fabric to stitched piece. Trim seam allowances; turn stitched piece right side out. Press top and bottom edges $\frac{1}{2}$" to wrong side of bellpull. Fold top and bottom edges 1$\frac{1}{2}$" to wrong side; whipstitch pressed edges to wrong side of bellpull and insert bellpull hardware.

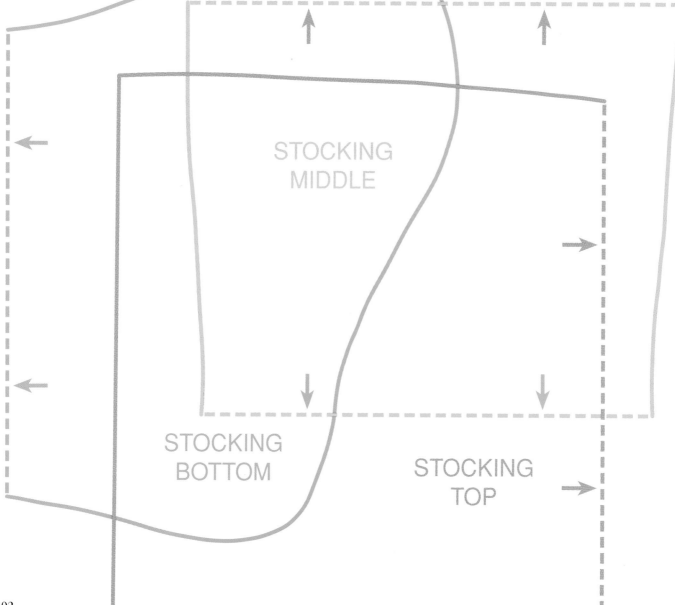

STOCKING MIDDLE

STOCKING BOTTOM

STOCKING TOP

FINISHING INSTRUCTIONS

Father Christmas, Little Lady's Christmas, Little Gent's Christmas, and Mr. Snowman and Friends Stockings (shown on pages 29, 36-37, and 39, charts on pages 76-77, 82-85, and 90-91).

For each stocking, you will need an 8" x 14" piece of fabric for backing, two 8" x 14" pieces of fabric for lining, 32" length of ¼" dia. purchased cording with attached seam allowance, 2" x 6" piece of fabric for hanger, tracing paper, and fabric marking pencil.

For stocking pattern, match arrows to form one pattern and trace pattern onto tracing paper; add a ½" seam allowance on all sides and cut out pattern. Referring to photo for placement, position pattern on wrong side of stitched piece; pin pattern in place. Use fabric marking pencil to draw around pattern; remove pattern and cut out on drawn line. Use pattern and cut **one** from backing fabric and **two** from lining fabric.

If needed, trim seam allowance of cording to ½". Matching raw edges, baste cording to right side of stocking front.

Matching right sides and leaving top edge open, use a ½" seam allowance to sew stitched piece and backing fabric together. Clip seam allowance at curves and turn stocking right side out. Press top edge of stocking ½" to wrong side.

Matching right sides and leaving top edge open, use a ⅝" seam allowance to sew lining pieces together; trim seam allowance close to stitching. **Do not turn lining right side out.** Press top edge of lining ½" to wrong side.

For hanger, press each long edge of fabric strip ½" to center. Matching long edges, fold strip in half and sew close to folded edges. Matching short edges, fold hanger in half and whipstitch to inside of stocking at left seam.

With wrong sides facing, place lining inside stocking; blind stitch lining to stocking.

Winter Fun Stocking (shown on page 38, chart on pages 90-91): For stocking, you will need a 13" x 6½" piece of fabric for cuff backing, two 8" x 17" pieces of fabric for stocking, two 8" x 17" pieces of fabric for lining, 2" x 6" piece of fabric for hanger, tracing paper, and fabric marking pencil.

Centering design horizontally with top of design 2" from one long edge of fabric, trim stitched piece to measure 13" x 6½".

For stocking cuff, match right sides and short edges; fold stitched piece in half. Using a ½" seam allowance, sew short edges together. Repeat for cuff backing.

Matching right sides, raw edges, and seams, use a ½" seam allowance to sew cuff and cuff backing together along lower edge of cuff; turn right side out and press. Baste cuff and cuff backing together close to raw edges.

For stocking pattern, match arrows of Stocking Pattern, page 92, to form one pattern and trace

pattern onto tracing paper; add a ½" seam allowance on all sides and cut out pattern. Matching right sides and raw edges, place stocking fabric pieces together; place pattern on fabric pieces and pin pattern in place. Use fabric marking pencil to draw around pattern; remove pattern and cut out on drawn line. Repeat with lining fabric pieces.

Matching right sides and leaving top edge open, use a ½" seam allowance to sew stocking pieces together. Clip seam allowance at curves and turn stocking right side out.

Matching right sides and leaving top edge open, use a ⅝" seam allowance to sew lining pieces together; trim seam allowance close to stitching. **Do not turn lining right side out.** With wrong sides facing, place lining inside stocking. Baste stocking and lining together close to raw edges.

Referring to photo and matching raw edges, place right side of cuff to inside of stocking with cuff back seam at center back of stocking. Use a ½" seam allowance to sew cuff and stocking together. Fold cuff 4½" to outside of stocking and press.

For hanger, press each long edge of fabric strip ½" to center. Matching long edges, fold strip in half and sew close to folded edges. Fold hanger in half, matching short edges; refer to photo and blind stitch to inside of stocking.

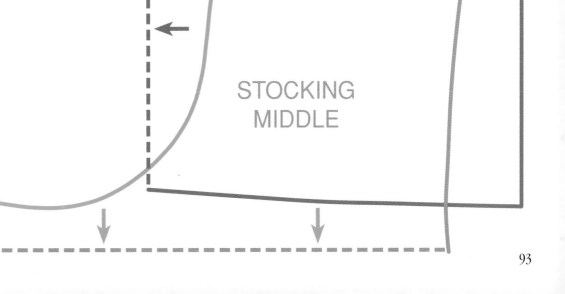

STOCKING
BOTTOM

STOCKING
TOP

STOCKING
MIDDLE

FINISHING INSTRUCTIONS

The Herald Angel, "Joy to the World", A Child Is Born, Merry Christmas Couple, Santa's Workshop, To All a Good Night, and Old-Time Sampler Stockings (shown on pages 7, 9, 11, 13, 15, 19, and 23, charts on pages 40-65 and 70-73).

For each stocking, you will need an 18" x 24" piece of fabric for backing, two 18" x 24" pieces of fabric for lining, 44" length of $^1/_4$" dia. purchased cording with attached seam allowance, 2" x 6" piece of fabric for hanger, tracing paper, and fabric marking pencil. For Old-time Sampler Stocking only, you will also need a $3^3/_4$" purchased tassel.

For stocking pattern, match arrows to form one pattern and trace pattern onto tracing paper; add a $^1/_2$" seam allowance on all sides and cut out pattern. Referring to photo for placement, position pattern on wrong side of stitched piece; pin pattern in place. Use fabric marking pencil to draw around pattern; remove pattern and cut out on drawn line. Use pattern and cut **one** from backing fabric and **two** from lining fabric.

If needed, trim seam allowance of cording to $^1/_2$". Matching raw edges, baste cording to right side of stocking front.

Matching right sides and leaving top edge open, use a $^1/_2$" seam allowance to sew stitched piece and backing fabric together. Clip seam allowance at curves and turn stocking right side out. Press top edge of stocking $^1/_2$" to wrong side.

Matching right sides and leaving top edge open, use a $^5/_8$" seam allowance to sew lining pieces together; trim seam allowance close to stitching. **Do not turn lining right side out.** Press top edge of lining $^1/_2$" to wrong side.

For hanger, press each long edge of fabric strip $^1/_2$" to center. Matching long edges, fold strip in half and sew close to folded edges. Matching short edges, fold hanger in half and whipstitch to inside of stocking at left seam.

With wrong sides facing, place lining inside stocking; blind stitch lining to stocking.

For Old-time Sampler Stocking, refer to photo and tack tassel to inside of stocking.

Sampler Border Stocking (shown on page 24, chart on pages 70-73): For stocking, you will need two 14" x 20" pieces of fabric for stocking, two 14" x 20" pieces of fabric for lining, 44" length of $^1/_2$" dia. purchased cording with attached seam allowance, $17^1/_2$" x $7^1/_2$" piece of fabric for cuff backing, 2" x 6" piece of fabric for hanger, $3^3/_4$" purchased tassel, tracing paper, and fabric marking pencil.

For stocking cuff, center design horizontally with top of design $1^1/_2$" from top edge of fabric; trim stitched piece to measure $17^1/_2$" x $7^1/_2$".

For stocking pattern, match arrows to form one pattern and trace pattern onto tracing paper; add a $^1/_2$" seam allowance on all sides and cut out pattern. Matching right sides and raw edges, place stocking fabric pieces together; place pattern on fabric pieces and pin pattern in place. Use fabric marking pencil to draw around pattern; remove pattern and cut out on drawn line. Repeat with lining fabric pieces.

If needed, trim seam allowance of cording to $^1/_2$". Matching raw edges, baste cording to right side of stocking front.

Matching right sides and leaving top edge open, use a $^1/_2$" seam allowance to sew stocking pieces together. Clip seam allowance at curves and turn stocking right side out.

Matching right sides and leaving top edge open, use a $^5/_8$" seam allowance to sew lining pieces together; trim seam allowance close to stitching. **Do not turn lining right side out.** With wrong sides facing, place lining inside stocking. Baste stocking and lining together close to top edge.

For stocking cuff, match right sides and short edges; fold cuff in half. Using a $^1/_2$" seam allowance, sew short edges together. Repeat for cuff backing.

Matching right sides, raw edges, and seams, use a $^1/_2$" seam allowance to sew cuff and cuff backing together along lower edge of cuff; turn right side out and press. Baste cuff and cuff backing together close to raw edges.

Referring to photo and matching raw edges, place right side of cuff to inside of stocking with cuff back seam at center back of stocking. Use a $^1/_2$" seam allowance to sew cuff and stocking together. Fold cuff 5" to outside of stocking and press.

For hanger, press each long edge of fabric strip $^1/_2$" to center. Matching long edges, fold strip in half and sew close to folded edges. Fold hanger in half, matching short edges; blind stitch to inside of stocking at left seam. Referring to photo, tack tassel to inside of stocking.

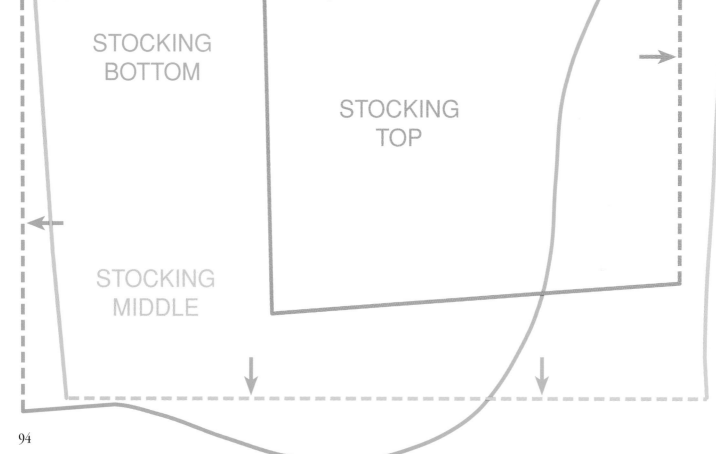

STOCKING
BOTTOM

STOCKING
TOP

STOCKING
MIDDLE

FINISHING INSTRUCTIONS

Opening His Pack Stocking (shown on page 21, chart and supplies on pages 66-69): For stocking pattern, match arrows to form one pattern and trace pattern onto tracing paper; add a ¹/₂" seam allowance on all sides and cut out pattern. Referring to photo for placement, position pattern on wrong side of stitched piece; pin pattern in place. Use fabric marking pencil to draw around pattern; remove pattern and cut out on drawn line. Use pattern and cut **one** from backing fabric and **two** from lining fabric.

If needed, trim seam allowance of cording to ¹/₂". Matching raw edges, baste cording to right side of stocking front.

Matching right sides and leaving top edge open, use a ¹/₂" seam allowance to sew stitched piece and backing fabric together. Clip seam allowance at curves and turn stocking right side out. Press top edge of stocking ¹/₂" to wrong side.

Matching right sides and leaving top edge open, use a ⁵/₈" seam allowance to sew lining pieces together; trim seam allowance close to stitching. **Do not turn lining right side out.** Press top edge of lining ¹/₂" to wrong side.

For hanger, press each long edge of fabric strip ¹/₂" to center. Matching long edges, fold strip in half and sew close to folded edges. Matching short edges, fold hanger in half and whipstitch to inside of stocking at left seam.

With wrong sides facing, place lining inside stocking; blind stitch lining to stocking.

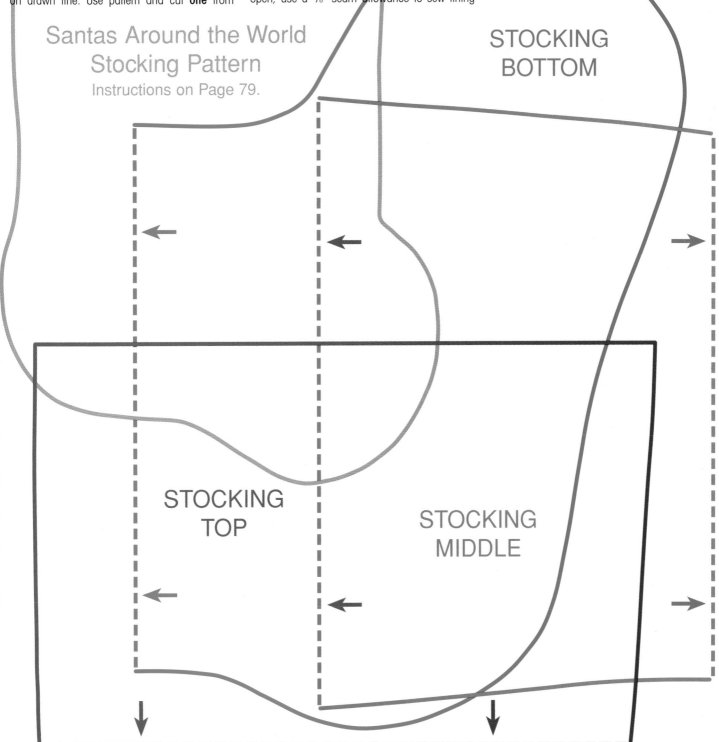

Santas Around the World
Stocking Pattern
Instructions on Page 79.

STOCKING BOTTOM

STOCKING TOP

STOCKING MIDDLE

GENERAL INSTRUCTIONS

WORKING WITH CHARTS

How to Read Charts: Each of the designs is shown in chart form. Each colored square on the chart represents one Cross Stitch or one Half Cross Stitch. Each colored triangle on the chart represents one Quarter Stitch. In some charts, reduced symbols are used to indicate Quarter Stitches (**Fig. 1**). **Fig. 2** and **Fig. 3** indicate Cross Stitch under Backstitch.

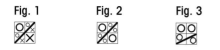

| **Fig. 1** | **Fig. 2** | **Fig. 3** |

Black or colored dots on the chart represent Cross Stitch or French Knots. The black or colored straight lines on the chart indicate Backstitch. The symbol is omitted or reduced when a French Knot or Backstitch covers a square.

Each chart is accompanied by a color key. This key indicates the color of floss to use for each stitch on the chart. The headings on the color key are for Cross Stitch (**X**), DMC color number (**DMC**), Quarter Stitch (**¼X**), Half Cross Stitch (**½X**), and Backstitch (**B'ST**). Color key columns should be read vertically and horizontally to determine type of stitch and floss color. Some designs may include stitches worked with metallic thread, such as blending filament or braid. The metallic thread may be blended with floss or used alone. If any metallic thread is used in a design, the color key will contain the necessary information.

STITCHING TIPS

Working over Two Fabric Threads: Use the sewing method instead of the stab method when working over two fabric threads. To use the sewing method, keep your stitching hand on the right side of the fabric (instead of stabbing the fabric with the needle and taking your stitching hand to the back of the fabric to pick up the needle). With the sewing method, you take the needle down and up with one stroke instead of two. To add support to stitches, it is important that the first Cross Stitch be placed on the fabric with stitch 1-2 beginning and ending where a vertical fabric thread crosses over a horizontal fabric thread (**Fig. 4**). When the first stitch is in the correct position, the entire design will be placed properly, with vertical fabric threads supporting each stitch.

Fig. 4

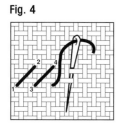

Working on Waste Canvas: Waste canvas is a special canvas that provides an evenweave grid for placing stitches on fabric. After the design is worked over the canvas, the canvas threads are removed, leaving the design on the fabric. The canvas is available in several mesh sizes.

Cover edges of canvas with masking tape. Cut a piece of lightweight non-fusible interfacing the same size as canvas to provide a firm stitching base.

Find desired stitching area and mark center of area with a pin. Match center of canvas to pin. Use the blue threads in canvas to place canvas straight on garment; pin canvas to garment. Pin interfacing to wrong side of garment. Baste all layers together as shown in **Fig. 5**.

Using a sharp needle, work design, stitching from large holes to large holes. Trim canvas to within ³/₄" of design. Dampen canvas until it becomes limp. Pull out canvas threads one at a time using tweezers (**Fig. 6**). Trim interfacing close to design.

Fig. 5	**Fig. 6**
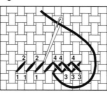	

STITCH DIAGRAMS

Note: Bring threaded needle up at 1 and all odd numbers and down at 2 and all even numbers.

Counted Cross Stitch (X): Work one Cross Stitch to correspond to each colored square on the chart. For horizontal rows, work stitches in two journeys (**Fig. 7**). For vertical rows, complete each stitch as shown (**Fig. 8**). When working over two fabric threads, work Cross Stitch as shown in **Fig. 9**. When the chart shows a Backstitch crossing a colored square (**Fig. 10**), a Cross Stitch should be worked first; then the Backstitch (**Fig. 15** or **16**) should be worked on top of the Cross Stitch.

Fig. 7	**Fig. 8**

Fig. 9	**Fig. 10**

Quarter Stitch (¼X): Quarter Stitches are denoted by triangular shapes of color on the chart and on the color key. For a Quarter Stitch, come up at 1 (**Fig. 11**), then split fabric thread to go down at 2. **Fig. 12** shows the technique for Quarter Stitches when working over two fabric threads.

Fig. 11	**Fig. 12**

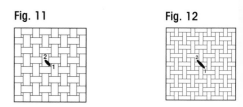

Half Cross Stitch (½X): This stitch is one journey of the Cross Stitch and is worked from lower left to upper right as shown in **Fig. 13**. When working over two fabric threads, work Half Cross Stitch as shown in **Fig. 14**.

Fig. 13	**Fig. 14**

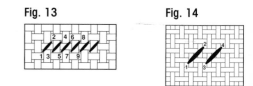

Backstitch (B'ST): For outline detail, Backstitch (shown on chart and on color key by black or colored straight lines) should be worked after the design has been completed (**Fig. 15**). When working over two fabric threads, work Backstitch as shown in **Fig. 16**.

Fig. 15	**Fig. 16**

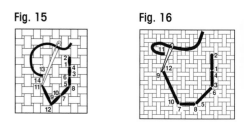

French Knot: Bring needle up at 1. Wrap floss once around needle and insert needle at 2, holding end of floss with non-stitching fingers (**Fig. 17**). Tighten knot, then pull needle through fabric, holding floss until it must be released. For larger knot, use more strands of floss; wrap only once.

Fig. 17

Instructions tested and photo items made by Arlene Allen, Lisa Arey, Kandi Ashford, Vicky Bishop, Alice Crowder, Muriel Hicks, Pat Johnson, Arthur Jungnickel, Phyllis Lundy, Susan McDonald, Patricia O'Neil, Angie Perryman, Laura Rowan, Stephanie Gail Sharp, Anne Simpson, Lavonne Sims, Lorissa Smith, Dawn C. Speer, Helen Stanton, and Trish Vines.